MW00510450

IN COMMAND

Visionary Author Tess Tims

Foreword Author Dr. Cheryl Wood

Foreword Author Patric Bradley

Expert Author Tye Miles

Expert Author Dr. Crystal Porter

Expert Author Angela Ellington

Copyright © 2021 by Little Publishing LLC
All rights reserved. No portion of this book may be reproduced, stored in
a retrieval system, or transmitted by any means electronic, mechanical,
photocopy recording, scanning, or other except brief quotations without
prior written permission of the publisher, except in case of brief
quotations embodied in critical reviews and certain other noncommerical
uses permitted by copyright law.

For permission requests, write to the publisher, addressed|
"Attention Permissions Coordinator," at aalittle08@gmail.com

Book Cover Design: Little Publishing LLC

Published By: Little Publishing LLC

ISBN: 978-1-7343314-4-8

TESS TIMS

A Message from the Visionary Author
Wrong Can Turn into Right
By: Tess Tims

Been there, done that, got the blazer.

In 2020 I was invited to tell my life story along with 29 other extraordinary leaders as a guest chapter for a book called *TRAILBLAZERS*. Now on the bestseller list, a success story of its own like the other unsinkable Trailblazer leaders/authors I had a certain defeat to stunning victory to share.

Wrong can turn to right.

My chapter celebrated my survival turnaround from disaster to rescue, prosperity and wellbeing, as I picked myself up from a devastating twist of fate, that tested my own grit and determination to the limits.

Inspired by the bravery, fellowship, and recognition of my earlier co-*Trailblazer*s, I am delighted to introduce my new selection of further commanding success stories. I have selected the chapters and authors from personal experience with *their* success stories on the betterment road to here in from 2020-2021.

And here too – we are all still shell-shocked and counting the damage in the maddening, muddling midst of COVID-19 19 where we face an entirely different world. It seems brazen to celebrate success in the light of such global suffering and distress. But I believe we are the very achievers who can apply the same ingenious survival skills we used before COVID-19 19, to bring about our own kind of transformative improvement for others during and after COVID-19 19.

That book is in the pipeline next but meanwhile we are here *now* IN COMMAND of the things we *can* control for which we are truly grateful.

COVID-19 19 and the new co-operation.

Post-COVID-19 19 First wave, on to Second wave, pre-vaccine 2020 - many brave souls were lost, some hospital battles won as courageous medical folk manned and womaned the front line to save our lives, while risking their own. Some immune systems mostly below 60 years old were triumphant in body defense, other immune systems above 60 years old were sadly compromised, as we as a world witnessed the sweeping global panic of overwhelming infection overtaking our lives.

Corona-coaster is no fun-fair ride.

From the shambles of that panic, the "corona-coaster" as Rockstar Pink called it, rocked our world with its crazy up and down and around the globe, causing devastation everywhere. It also generated neighborly adaptability, voluntary assistance, and charitable support. Citizens started to change where the common enemy became the illness, and many former enemies became alliances overnight.

In the midst of all this chaos, humankind was transforming itself. Many lost their jobs in lockdown, in some countries far more women than men, and others were forced to create innovative business models to endure. Ingenuity and self-sufficiency ruled.

Those of our people still alive who remember World Wars, the duration, and the troubled aftermath, relate the menace of Corona disease to those troubled times and as everyday heroes urge us to stand firm and show the same grit and forbearance in the face of radical world change.

Transformation again keeps us one step ahead from catastrophe. Innovative, prepared, protective we stand, then change, then stand again. One tiny virus took giant steps into our homes and our lives.

With tenacity that was hard for humankind to beat, and an ever-growing infection rate more so in cold climates, the virus appears to mutate faster than the best of us can. And if ever a vital catch-up was needed, the order of the day is human inventiveness and initiative. Change was and is the kingpin in our global first aid kit.

You cannot be truly positive till you have looked deeply at the negative.

All this reflection on the pain and fear and helplessness in the face of COVID-19 19, takes me back to the pain and suffering and confusion I felt when I first started on my journey to adulthood and a rewarding future for myself. There I was, an honor-roll scholar - unexpectedly pregnant at 17, bound not for college as I had eagerly planned then (my family revered education, a college degree was everything) but single motherhood, financial strain, and apartness from my graduating peers. And as I saw it, the shame of Welfare. The end of the world for me. Not to mention the very worst experience to follow, homelessness and banishment from my family.

The same old story needed a new ending.

I was the golden apple of my father's eye, only daughter, his proverbial good princess. From that exalted place I fell for the proverbial bad boy as does every good girl at least once in her life. My military-man dad, rule-bound, who had forbidden the relationship from the start caught us on a forbidden date one night. He threw me out of my home and family and mind and straight into the arms of the boy he did not want me to have in the first place.

Bad boy offered me somewhere to stay, as I'd nowhere else to go. Then we added someone else to my bad move. A baby. My daughter.

Devastated to be cut off from my close-knit family (my mom and brothers helped in the background; my father angry for a time in the foreground). Birth was imminent. Thankfully, a doctor family friend offered to waive the fees on my required C-section delivery on condition that I promised to attend college afterwards.

A promising student like me – I could not promise fast enough.

Reluctantly I went on welfare. With some secret family funding from my mother's side, a history of excellent grades and all-round student recommendations, and eventually a fatherly pardon, my baby daughter and I returned to my family home, all of us transformed in time by the magic of a darling new child. Part-time income on the side coupled with college studies and child-raising consumed me, along with the determination that no matter what, I would one day own my own home. And that homelessness would never, ever appear on my testimonial again.

Transformation thrives in chaos, I learned to make it work for me.

Transformation, as I always say, in my popular 3C's lectures thrives in chaos. And like my 3C students I was about find out how I was next going to thrive.

In my own life for example I took 6 years to get my Computer Science degree as I studied and single-mothered. The multi-tasking was chaotic, but I was becoming used to change and I transformed my family unit to Houston to a secure (a logical assumption) job at NASA and worked there for 7 years.

There I was, a safe landing at NASA, according to plan.

Then overnight unplanned for chaos – as John Lennon famously once said: Life happens while you are busy making other plans. Retrenchment, a fancy way of saying we cannot afford you anymore. Sorry. But as the saying goes: Sorry does not pay the bills.

The space program saved on space – my office.

Professionally I held back the let-go tears, then when I got home, I had to let-go on the let-go. Opportunity knocked. Luckily through all the crying and sighing, I heard it and took the knock. Or my brother did.

"Retrenchment's you're opening to something new; something you. You are not just a logical scientist. Go do something creative that makes you happy. Something you have always wanted to do. Fashion, maybe. Glamour. Just reinvent yourself", he said in that bossy but right way that older brothers have. And as a card-carrying member of my entrepreneurial family, (work ethic revered along with education), and all us kids used to summer vacation jobs of dizzying variety, I took the leap.

As they say jump and the safety net will appear. They were right. And the safety net profits soon started appearing in my bank account.

Airspace to hairspace almost overnight.

In my case, I cut from rocket launches to the launch of my own hair salon. Airspace to hairspace with TnT (Tess Tims Transformation and Training – all those T's gave me my A-game. Work atmosphere was a blast. Business rocketed.

When I passed the stringent TessTest (I really like my name and slip it in to play wherever I can) initial training and the further training which my Tess-driver self-insisted was required of me to be the best, (I was on a training train, stopping at all useful salon stations) and the super-training beyond that, to cut, color and excel in my own wonderful Ash Blond perfection that really should win gold. Still competing with Tess against Tess, I extended myself even more.

Cut to my famous hair extension skills to the Stars.

It was ironic that this former NASA scientist once involved in the quest of star travel would have found a way to have the Stars travel to *her*.

For my hair-extensions styled so beautifully I was getting the greatest hairpiece of the local action.

The roots of all this activity? In my case from outer space to inner peace, I can see now that I became *everything,* I was cut out to be. Tessed for success or even Tressed for success (I told you I loved my name) was exactly how I saw myself.

I refer now to the dictionary (my other good book)

Transformation - definition: the induced or spontaneous change of one element into another.

That is how Science sees it, and a lesson to you and me. Remember though, whether spontaneous or induced, change taking place can be chaotic or it would not be change. What I jokingly think of as transformation.

Transformation or tranceformation?

The upside is whether you want wide-awake transformation or the half-asleep transformation – it is going to happen anyway. Afterwards, like it or not, you will find yourselves in your *new element.* What you personally do with that element has the potential to light up your life, your brain, and your balance sheet.

New elements. My Testimonial.

1. My new elements I have learned to embrace with change are:

2. From Welfare to Well-Educated ~ I raised my daughter singlehandedly and raised my game against all odds for a Bachelor of Science degree.

3. At NASA from the get-go as a Computer Scientist, to cutbacks let go after 7 years.

4. Fired up by my own firing, I took a hair-raising gamble to do what I had always secretly dreamed of.

5. I went to Beauty School. (as a committed mom who was there to learn and work, not party, more interested in glamorous than amorous).

6. I brought my Scientific skills to the chaotic hard to-break-even beauty business.

7. The outstanding $42 water bill one month landed me in hot water (one start-out penniless period), but the money gushed in and I survived.

8. With a head, face, and heart for beauty, I built a hair styling empire, going to great lengths to specialize in the art of celebrity hair

extensions. I offered my exclusive Beauty Preuner program that taught my students to recruit 100 new clients in 30 days. I am a self-made millionaire today and transformation plus hard work got me here.

9.   With the financial drought of 2009, the wash out of expensive hairdos in Texas, I was almost washed up.

10. A hair's breadth escape was my change to online hairdressing training.

11. I started an international radio station called the Tess Zone, transmitted to 136 countries.

12. Radio chatting/interviewing got me interested in training to be a good speaker.

13. On my way to a cross-state speaking engagement, an unexpected flood nearly downed me, water-wise and with PTSD afterwards. The following year I delivered my lost speech online. And a tip from me to you, always check the weather before you drive.

14. A handsome man turned ugly is another kind of "whether" check.

15. A successful transformation speaker and coach is one that makes you hold on to your seats. I am a coach and not a slow one by far…

16. A mover and shaker is an influencer.

Your rescue team. You, Yourself, Aye. Go team!

Sometimes you must buckle on your shining armor alone, rev up that horsepower with your heels and ride valiantly to your own defense. Despite the gloom and shadows and the scaredy-cat inside of you versus the big, bad boogeymen outside (never compare your inside with another is outside), you absolutely CAN pull yourself out of that dark hole.

Remember meds and counseling are helpful if needed. You can dust yourself off, except for the Stardust of course, where you are going, you are going to need that. Climb right back into the driver's seat to where you were headed – the top of your chosen field.

Your field can change so clear those fences.

Transformation being the true offspring of chaos, as I mention constantly, may cause you to find yourself in a completely different field from the one you started with. A field that not only grows along with you. But as new directions crop up, introduces vibrant new growth you never even dreamed of.

But only because you ploughed up the old and planted the new, only because of Transformation.

Soon you will be wise enough to harvest your growth.

That wisdom comes from flexibility. Flexibility is the helpmate of transformation, as it can unscramble your chaos into a new opportunity, a possibility of an entirely different direction in a manner sometimes alarmingly shocking and breathtaking. Other times it can be painfully obvious. You may ask yourself "why didn't I see that? what was I thinking?", but of course you did not know then what you do now.

Look ahead. You are right here on the hair-trigger of change.

You are wondering how to take the bits and pieces you are left with to assemble a new take for your next life (no, I do not mean Heaven, although succeeding at what feels wonderful to you *is* heavenly), birthed in the renewal of Transformation. Admittedly the labor can be painful. But fortunately, there is a doula nearby.

Me.
Tess Tims.
Transformation Trainer
Here to assist, with my own brand of **TnT.**
Explosive, but not harmful.

Because I do not create chaos, I transform it.

tess@teachmetess.com
(832) 368-9383
Linktr.ee/TessTims

About Tess Tims

Tess Tims is an ordinary woman who has accomplished truly extraordinary things. She started out as an unmarried teen mother on welfare, with no savings, no skills and no connections. At one point she could not even pay a $42 water bill. Then she transformed herself. She put herself through college, earned a Bachelor of Science degree and worked at NASA for years.

Today Tess runs a thriving mini empire. She is a topTransformational coach, a best-selling author and a sought- after speaker. She helps women and licensed hairstylists to become AYE-Sayers by sharing her Me, Myself and AYE attitude, through her 3C's life improvement course and her beauty-preneur program.

Tess also runs a very successful beauty salon and is a recognized industry leader in spiritually rewarding hair replacement services, for women who suffer hair loss from burns, chemo andAlopecia. To reach even more people with her life-transforming message, Tess added live Facebook and Instagram feeds and hosts a regular radio podcast called The Tess Zone airing exclusively on her new network - Tess Zone Broadcasts. Billed as the hurtin', cryin', cheatin', lyin radio show – it more than lives up to its name.

Listen to Tess Tims Today, and Transform Yourself

tess@teachmetess.com

www.tesstims.com

Table of Contents

DR. CHERYL WOOD

Foreword Author
By: Dr. Cheryl Wood

The hard reality that each of us must face on our journey of life is that we will unquestionably encounter a barrage of unexpected punches along the journey – challenges, obstacles, roadblocks and setbacks – that are designed to hold us hostage to who we are and prevent us from stepping into the person we have the power to become. *IN COMMAND,* presented by powerhouse Tess Tims, a successful businesswoman, trailblazer and global leader, and a cohort of dynamic co-authors serves as a brilliant reminder that we are in full control of our own destiny and that we never have to settle for being the sum of the negative experiences we have faced in life. Instead, we can choose to be *IN COMMAND* of our lives, to be resilient, tenacious, unstoppable, and refuse to be broken by the things designed to break us. Although we are sometimes battered and bruised by life's challenges, we can ultimately choose to bounce-back from anything that knocks us down. As collectively expressed throughout this book by all of the co-authors, every obstacle we face has the power to build character, create greater strength, liberate us physically, spiritually and emotionally, and move us closer to who we are truly destined to be. And our challenges and setbacks simply become a part of a bigger story that we get to share in order to inspire others on their journey.

As you delve deep into the stories penned as a part of *IN COMMAND,* you will feel motivated, inspired and empowered to find the power and purpose in every situation you experience in life. You will begin to peel back the layers of who you are even when faced with challenges and obstacles and discover how you can leverage every obstacle to manifest what your heart truly desires.

After reading *IN COMMAND*, you will feel refreshed and reenergized as you are reminded that you have everything it takes to boldly overcome any toxic beliefs about who you can become and what you can accomplish in spite of where you start or how many times you get knocked down along the way.

IN COMMAND will touch you at your core as it speaks to the real emotions that most of us experience at some point in our lives when we face heart-wrenching trials and tribulations that we wish we could escape in the moment. You will feel a genuine connection to each co-author as they are completely vulnerable and transparent in sharing their raw, authentic truth. The emboldened belief that *you are enough to turn any obstacle in your favor and come out as a VICTOR* is woven throughout the pages of this inspirational book and is like a breath of fresh air!

If you are craving to live your life with increased purpose, intention, joy, and meaning, *IN COMMAND* promises to feed your soul with much needed confirmation that you have everything it takes to be persistent, consistent and courageous as you stay in the fight to pursue your dreams and live a life of abundance. As reminded in each chapter, you can expect that any level of success in your life will be accompanied by challenges, roadblocks, obstacles and setbacks, but as so eloquently expressed by one of the *IN COMMAND* co-authors, "Have faith that you can follow your dreams, you will run into obstacles but keep moving forward toward your destiny."

Tess Tims has outdone herself in spearheading this encouraging compilation. She has compiled a host of real-life stories from individuals of diverse ages, backgrounds and walks of life as a powerful resource that will impact, influence and positively transform lives globally. *IN COMMAND* will feel like a priceless gift to every person who reads it.

I implore you to sit in a quiet space and fully reflect on the lessons shared in this dynamic book. Open your mind and your heart to embrace the experiences of each co-author, and allow the belief that you have a right to be IN COMMAND of your life to penetrate your soul!

About Dr. Cheryl Wood

Dr. Cheryl Wood is an international empowerment speaker, 11x best-selling author, leadership expert, and master speaker development coach. She equips entrepreneurs with the tools to unleash the power of their voice, share the transformational impact of their story, and monetize their expertise. Dr. Wood has trained countless leaders & influencers across the U.S. and abroad in South Africa, India, France, United Kingdom, Canada and the Bahamas, to name a few. She empowers entrepreneurs to get out of their comfort zone, take calculated risks, and create a living legacy.

Dr. Wood has been featured on ABC, Radio One, Forbes Magazine, Huffington Post, ESSENCE, Black Enterprise, Good Morning Washington, Fox 5 News, Fox 45 News, The Washington Informer, The Baltimore Times, Afro-American Newspaper and numerous other media outlets. She has delivered keynote presentations for a host of large and small organizations including NASA, the FBI, U.S. Department of Defense, U.S. Department of Agriculture, The United Nations, Verizon, Federally Employed Women, Blacks In Government, Women's Council of Realtors, the Congressional Black Caucus and the National Association of Legal Professionals.

www.CherylEmpowers.com

PATRIC BRADLEY

Foreword Author
By: Patric Bradley

Defeat is not in the vocabulary!!

I have been in the beauty business for over 25 years and I have loved every year of it. I have owned my product and tool line since 2008 (Pelement Products) sold at www.patricbradley.com. I have seen ups and downs and downs and ups throughout. Success is very simple. Kill the defeat bug!! You must study your market and become great in it no matter what. You can no longer strive to just be good, greatness or nothing. Study your competition and try and beat them across the board. Your goal should be to stay ahead of them by 5 steps. Action is key and staying innovative is a must . LEAVE THE EXCUSES AT HOME IF YOU CAN'T BE GREAT!!

Note: Know that some things require a team effort; you cannot be great by yourself. I have earned millions in and out of my industry and I strive for EXCELLENCE every day I wake up. Getting up early is the first step. Why? Because sleep is the new BROKE! Defeat is not the worst of failures; to not have tried is the true failure. Instead of dwelling upon what went wrong, try to focus your attention on what you can do right the next go-round. Remind yourself that defeat is a part of greatness. Some common synonyms of defeat: overcome, conquer, overthrow, vanquish. While all these words mean "to get better "defeat does not mean finality or completeness of vanquish which it otherwise equals.

Defeat is the opposite of victory. When you lose, you suffer defeat. When defeat comes, accept it as a signal that your plans are not sound, rebuild those plans and set sail once more toward your ultimate goal.

Now that we understand defeat a little more let us move on. I am Patric Bradley and I have seen defeat almost my entire life, with every defeat I suffered I had to find out what went wrong and fix it. Period! Defeat comes when we want SUCCESS, but we do not want it bad enough to go beyond what the competition is already doing. Giving 100% will no longer get you to the winners' circle. Whatever you decide to be in life - athlete, business owner, doctor, lawyer, singer, engineer, hairstylist, etc. You must have a plan and 80% of that plan needs to be ACTION. Action is very important and probably more important than the plan. Your drive must be on 1000%. Failure is not an option. Winning is the goal and excuses are not on the menu.

This amazing book was designed to showcase others who have faced defeat and turned it completely around. Defeat is not the end of the road and Tess Tims has put together and amazing book, *IN COMMAND*. Ever since I have known Tess, she has had crazy enthusiasm and a drive to become successful. Everything she tries has success. She studied, researched, and put in the work to become great. Tess is one of those go over and beyond girls and that is what it takes to be IN COMMAND.

About Patric Bradley

HAIRSTYLIST | EDUCATOR | MAKEUP ARTIST | PHOTOGRAPHER

World renowned beauty expert Patric Antonio Bradley has been acknowledged as a beauty industry icon for two decades. His God-given talent inspires and enables him to be innovative and imaginative while creating trendsetting hairstyles and show stopping makeovers. Capturing the attention of artists around the globe, his bold styles have been featured by Dudley products, Farouk Systems, and Naked by Essations, just to name a few. He was also the Artistic Director for Dudley Products, and Creative Director for Farouk Systems. His work has been displayed on more than 80 national and international magazine covers and billboards around the globe.

Other accolades include winning more than 30 national and international hair and makeup competitions, including the prestigious "Top Stylist and Educator" honor at Bronner Brothers International Beauty Show in 2017, and numerous other awards. where he now serves as chairman of judges for the Bronner Bros. Hair Battle Royale. Patric can be seen in the movie *Good Hair* and authored "All Dressed Up and No Hair To Do" and "Makeup for Women of Color". He has also won an innumerable amount of "beauty education" awards. The Beauty industry appreciates and recognizes Patric's hard work, prowess and expertise; therefore he is considered one of the top 10 artists in the country.

To add another notch to his belt, in 2007 Patric Bradley started his own styling team, *Team Hollywood*; and his professional product line, *P Element*, in 2008. His latest venture is a partnership with Naked Essations bringing an industry game changer and newest collaboration, *Naked* and *Patric Antonio Bradley So Soft Relaxer*. He travels around the world expounding his haircutting, coloring, hairstyling skills and sharpening his craft as an international editorial photographer for stylist around the world. His imagination as a hairstylist and makeup artist knows no boundaries. His funkiness and free-flowing creativity is depicted by *Team Hollywood*. He sets out to have one of the top teams and companies in the

7

country. Patric Bradley recently started Rho Delta Tau, a Greek organization for hairstylist. Rho Delta Tau is an organization that provides for the less fortunate, as well as provides relief to those affected by acts of nature, as well as contribute to other charities.

Patric Bradley continues to make an impact by instructing hairstyling and makeup at interactive hair shows and events throughout the world. His credentials include educating at the International Beauty Show (IBS), Bronner Brothers, Americas Beauty Show (ABS), Spectrum Beauty Expo, IHS, and Premiere Shows. He is also an acclaimed photographer, photographing for some of the best stylists and top magazines in the country and abroad.

Like any knowledgeable teacher, Patric stays abreast and keeps his skills "on point" by working tirelessly in Houston, Texas. Patric Bradley is an artist who sets the bar high and paves the way for "cutting edge" trends in hairstyling, education and makeup for years to come with his unique and captivating creativity.

TYE MILES

Expert Author

**Approval Seeking: The Silent Killer of Success
and How To Overcome It**

By: Tye Miles

"Never sacrifice your authenticity for the approval of others."
~ Unknown

Approval seeking is like a killer drug. It can become an addiction, and you quickly develop a need for more. When you have a toxic need for approval, you value others' beliefs, opinions, and needs above your own. Other people's opinion outweighs your view of yourself. In our culture, social media makes it easy to get hooked on this addictive behavior. Your entire decision making process is eventually taken over by your need for the approval of others. The thought of being rejected or receiving disapproval becomes an emotionally painful experience. You have a hard time making decisions and taking decisive action without other's approval. You forfeit your right to express your own individuality for the sake of conforming to the expectations of others. Perpetuating this cycle of sacrificing your own needs, dreams, and ambitions to have their approval or avoid conflict. Amongst the negative consequences of approval-seeking behaviors are:

- Settling for less in terms of your goals and achievement
- Lowered sense of personal fulfillment and happiness
- Decreased levels of self-esteem and confidence
- Mediocre performance and procrastination
- Increased internal conflict and stress

Sounds familiar? Most of us go through this phase of life at one point or another. Habitual patterns like these are usually tell-tell signs of approval seeking. As a result, slowly but surely causing one to change their actions, attitude, and behavior to be accepted or to avoid being rejected by others. And it is because of this common reality that many are forfeiting their happiness, highest potential, and well-being and finding themselves living beneath what they believe is possible for their lives. In this chapter, I will show you how to *recognize* your own approval-seeking habit, some common *origins* for seeking approval (people-pleasing), and how to *overcome* this success trap blocking your success and ability to live a life of your own choosing.

Take this quick Approval Seeking Assessment to help identify your current approval-seeking behaviors. Answer Yes or No to the questions below.

Yes   No

☐   ☐   Do you change or shrink your position because someone seems to disapprove?

☐   ☐   Do you often feel inadequate because you think you do not measure up to others in terms of talent, success, social status, or intelligence?

☐   ☐   Do you feel you cannot make decisions for your own life because you are obligated to live up to the expectations of others?

☐   ☐   Do you feel worried, upset, or insulted when or if you think someone disagrees with you?

☐   ☐   Do you put others' needs above your own, so your needs are the last to be met or are never met? And do you feel you do not know what your real needs are?

☐ ☐ Do you find that, regardless of how much public or social approval you receive, you still feel unhappy, unfulfilled, or undeserving?

☐ ☐ Do you express agreement (verbal or nonverbal) when you disagree?

☐ ☐ Do you do things you do not want to do because you are afraid to say no?

☐ ☐ Do you find yourself apologizing for how you feel even when others have not expressed disapproval?

☐ ☐ Do you ever pretend to know something you do not because you are afraid to admit you do not?

☐ ☐ Do you behave in any way contrary to your identity, purpose, and core values?

The need to seek approval is something that starts in childhood and echoes throughout life. Just think about it. As a child, you were rewarded when you did what your guardian said was right and disciplined for what your guardian said was wrong. As a result, you, like me, did more of the right things according to what they believed was "right" and less of the things they believed were "wrong." You were being conditioned all your life to fit into the expectations of what your family, teachers, employers, community, society, and this world deemed acceptable for you.

You may argue that you do not engage in approval-seeking behavior. However, there are common behaviors which you may fail to see as approval seeking. Sometimes these compromises show up to keep the peace, or because the matter at hand is really not important to you, or maybe it's useful to you to let others have their way, so you keep silent, making you susceptible to this approval-seeking pattern. When these behaviors happen too often or are solely motivated by a need for approval, you are adopting an unhealthy behavior that leads to negative outcomes in your life or business.

Here are some examples of the impact of approval-seeking in the lives of real women I've worked with over the years:

- That career she wanted but didn't pursue in her youth because her parents disapproved seemed out of reach at the age of 50, so she started convincing herself that what she was doing was good enough, yet was unsatisfied.

- That business idea she kept putting off until the kids were grown because she felt they needed her more. Now they're grown, and yet she still has no business plans.

- The organization she carried in her heart, but she felt she needed others to validate her idea before she could move forward.

- That desire to increase the prices for her services, but she was afraid people would reject her offer or question the value of her services. So, she continued charging beneath her worth, sabotaging the financial health and growth of her business.

- The wife who limited her own ambitions because she was afraid that her husband would feel threatened by her success.

- The teen mom trying too hard in life to prove to others that she was enough.

If you can relate, then I know you fully understand how this unhealthy behavior has been negatively impacting your life and will continue until you learn how to overcome it. So, how do you begin to break free of this unhealthy need to seek approval and take more command of your own life? In my book, *Woman Own Your BS!*, I breakdown the following ten steps to help women (and men, too) break free from people-pleasing (approval seeking) so that they can continue to be helpful to others without sacrificing their own needs, diminishing their dreams, and compromising their core values. These ten steps are:

Step 1   Stop Waiting for Permission

Most people live their entire life based on what someone else thinks about them: what they wear, what they eat, what they drink, what they listen to, who they hang with, where they live, what they drive, how they wear their hair, what lipstick color they wear, what picture to post, and what to say on said post.

But the truth is, other people's opinions of us are none of our business. Their opinions have absolutely nothing to do with us and everything to do with them, their beliefs, values, past experiences, judgments, expectations, likes, and dislikes.

You don't need permission to be authentic, ambitious, bold, courageous, and brilliant.

Step 2   Acknowledge Your Need for Validation

Honestly, acknowledging the level of your need for approval allows you to become aware of how approval seeking has dictated your behavior in various areas of your life and work.

If you only grasp one thing, let it be this; you don't need other people to like everything about you, everything you do, or always agree with you! If your habit of people-pleasing is left unchecked, you will forfeit your own success and happiness.

Step 3   Identify Where It All Began

Having a high need for approval is typically caused by underlying feelings of inadequacy, which motivates your need for others' approval.

Typically, this behavior starts early in life. Maybe it began in childhood with a desire to make your parents feel proud, or perhaps you had a difficult time making friends in school and became fearful of rejection as a result. As an adult, perhaps a superior rejected a presentation or project you worked on. Or maybe you failed to live up to someone's expectations or your own's.

Instead of seeking the approval of others or trying to prove your worth, taking the time to reflect on your upbringing and even adulthood may help you identify the factors that contribute to your need to seek approval.

Step 4   Accept Yourself As-Is

No more defining who you are by whom you're with or what you have. Realize that you don't need anyone to tell you how amazing you are or to make you happy. Admittedly, it feels very good to have others compliment you; however, you MUST know who you are and be happy when they don't.

Accept yourself as-is, including your own gifts, talents, and abilities! Honor the brilliance and value you bring to every relationship you have. The world needs you—your personality, intellect, and all that energy and uniqueness you bring.

Step 5   Stop Comparing Yourself

When you compare yourself to others, you tend to diminish the value of your own skills, talents, and abilities, causing you to feel less than. So, stop it.

Comparison makes you believe you're not good enough. It will make you believe what you're doing isn't good enough—like you don't matter—until not just your head believes but even worse, your heart too. It causes you to stay stuck or feel like giving up long before you even get started. It prevents you from experiencing the freedom of genuinely loving yourself fully and compassionately without competing with anyone or anything else.

Step 6   Build Your Own Woman *(or man)*

To build your own woman *(or man)*, first look within yourself and honestly evaluate the areas of your life that do not excite you, where you feel dissatisfied and inauthentic. From there, you must know what goals you want to accomplish, and then for each goal, list any beliefs you can think of that might be holding you back. Then question those beliefs one by one and create new empowering beliefs to replace them. Building your own woman *(or man)* starts within, on the belief level, and then on the action level, therefore, manifesting what you want in terms of your conditions, circumstances, and environments.

Step 7   Release Limiting Beliefs

Release limiting beliefs that have been causing you to get in your own way and holding you back from reaching your goals. To become the woman *(or man)* you want to be and create the life you want to live, you must identify the beliefs that limit you and release them so that you can move forward.

Limiting beliefs are those specific stories we tell ourselves that hold us back in some way from becoming the woman *(or man)* we genuinely want to be.

Step 8   Calling in The New

You must replace each limiting belief with an empowering one representing the new story you will tell yourself about your own abilities, relationships, finances, and dreams. Empowering beliefs support you in reaching your goals and enable you to enjoy a more satisfying life. I refer to this process as *calling in the new*. During this process, you can choose to replace your old limiting beliefs with beliefs that empower you and are in alignment with the life you wish to create and enjoy.

Step 9   Protecting the New

As a people-pleaser, you most likely struggle with setting boundaries, and it has created challenges in many areas of your life. Learning to protect the commitment you've made to become your own first priority by setting boundaries will be a major adjustment, and you will definitely experience growing pains. This step is rather revealing, and you'll soon recognize those people who genuinely care about your happiness and goals and the nature of your relationships.

This is your chance to develop a nurturing, supportive relationship with yourself without putting up a public facade and people-pleasing.

Step 10 Integration for Transformation

Changing your beliefs can be unsettling at first. So, do not set yourself up for failure by trying to transform your whole life in one day. The power of this work does not happen overnight. Integrating new empowering beliefs is a simple process that can quite literally change your reality. All it takes is time and practice. Simply look for ways to transform your beliefs into behaviors, even if you have to push past your old lingering tendencies to shrink, hide, and hold back. Remember, transforming your life happens one belief, one decision, and one action at a time.

Conclusion

It takes a helluva lot of courage to embrace your individuality and live according to your own core values and beliefs. Respecting your own authenticity and pursuing your boldest goals will require you to avoid approval-seeking behaviors. Everyone will not like you, agree with you, or understand your vision for your life (including business). Failing to address approval-seeking behavior can lead to passive-aggressive behavior and a mediocre life. You can learn to overcome approval-seeking behavior with Tye's easy-to-follow book that will guide you to being, doing, thinking, believing, behaving, and engaging life in a way that enables you to become the woman you want while creating a life you love.

At the end of my coaching sessions, I always ask my clients to share their biggest aha moments they want to remember from their session. It helps them mentally grasp the most significant insight valuable to their growth. So, I'm curious, what's been most helpful for you from this chapter? **What is the most meaningful action you will take because of reading this chapter? I'd love to hear your answer! You can share it with me at tye@tyemiles.com.**

I personally read every message and can't wait to hear from you!

Tye Miles - Certified Personal Coach, Business Strategist, Personal Branding Expert, International Speaker, Metaphysician & Entrepreneur. She is the creator of the personal development brand, FierceHER Woman, and the founder of Women's Well-Being Firm. After 15 years as a successful entrepreneur in the beauty industry and earning millions as a hairstylist and salon owner, Tye decided to sell her salon to further align her work with her life purpose and what she is most passionate about – women empowerment and entrepreneurship.

Her mission: To empower women and women entrepreneurs to create a meaningful life aligned with their personal values, passion, and purpose.

Specializing in online visibility and business growth strategy, along with spiritual success principles, positive psychology coaching and neurolinguistic techniques, Tye supports her clients to express their authenticity, leverage their expertise, challenge their fears, and take risks necessary to attain their boldest life and business goals. Tye is unique with her transparent, energetic, and practical training style that inspires her audience into action.

To learn more about Tye, her services, or book her for your event, visit www.wwbfirm.com.

About Tye Miles

Tye Miles is a Certified Personal Coach, Business Strategist, Personal Branding Expert, International Speaker, and Entrepreneur. She is the creator of personal development brand, FierceHer Woman and founder of Women's Well-Being Firm and Wood & Royalty Jewelry.

Tye's Passion:

To empower women entrepreneurs to build, launch and grow profitable brands and businesses. Specializing in online visibility and business growth and strategy, along with spiritual success principles, positive psychology coaching and neurolinguistic techniques. She supports her clients to leverage their authenticity, own their personal power, challenge their fears, and take the risks necessary to attain their boldest goals.

Tye is unique with her transparent, energetic, and actionable training style that inspires her audience into action.

CRYSTAL E. PORTER, PH.D.

Expert Author
A Legacy of Disruption – Using Fear as Fuel
By: Crystal E. Porter, Ph.D.

I knew I was pregnant. You know how you have an overwhelming feeling that something is true before you have any proof? The knowledge didn't come upon me with any sense of dread or foreboding; it just fell in my mind like any other fact I'd gathered. I was pregnant, and in three months, I was set to travel to the Ozarks and start a doctorate program in Chemistry.

Disruption - a break or interruption in the normal course or continuation of some activity, process.

Can I tell you how afraid I was? I was young, unwed, pregnant and would be traveling to a place where few people looked like me and entering a rigorous program guaranteed to be challenging for anyone, but especially a Black woman. The easy thing would have been to defer my acceptance, put a hold on my academic pursuits until after the baby was born. Most people agreed that it was the right thing to do. When I kept planning my departure, people thought I was crazy. I wasn't crazy. I also wasn't a stereotype – a young woman with so much potential sidelined by an unplanned pregnancy. I would not fall prey to that system.

I was a disruptor.

I was fearful, but I followed my passion for studying science. When I think about it now, I wonder how I felt so confident. The fact is, I didn't. I didn't know what I was doing; I was terrified. I wasn't sure how any of my plans would work, but I knew that I was going to try, and whatever problems arose, I'd tackle them one at a time. That is a secret of moving beyond the status quo—you don't have to know everything to begin; you just start.

I started by focusing on my work, making a schedule, and building my network. I was blessed to have the support of my family and friends as well as my baby's father, now my husband of over 25 years, to help. I created a life for myself, and when my baby was born, we named her Nia, which means *purpose*. It was a perfect name because it expressed an underlying truth about myself and my feelings toward my new daughter. Purpose.

The backbone of my being able to make a life for myself as a budding scientist in Missouri and bring to existence this beautiful girl was my sense of purpose. Despite my fear, I felt an overwhelming desire to succeed as a chemist. As I drove home with Nia, I knew that providing for her health and well-being only strengthened this purpose. In the end, I graduated as the first Black person with a Ph.D. in Chemistry from the University of Rolla – Missouri (now, Missouri State University of Science & Technology).

I immediately received an offer from one of the top producers of consumer goods in the US as a senior research scientist. It was a tough job. Again, people questioned how I would be able to manage my family and my career. Both my husband and I had high demanding jobs that required frequent travel. Stereotypes would suggest that I pull my goals back to take care of our young family, but that would not work for us. My husband and I always had each other's back when it came to career opportunities and taking care of our children. We sat and came up with a plan that involved my mother retiring and coming to live with us. While this did alleviate some of the pressure, I still struggled with my responsibility to my home and my career.

I loved my career and the impact my colleagues and I were making on ethnic hair research. I was charged with leading a physics team developing new methods to understand the effects of products on hair and obtain knowledge about curly hair from all over the world. At the same time, I was committed to showing my girls that success wasn't only about a big title. I had to make hard decisions and show up for them during critical times so that they would know that an absent mother was unacceptable. Even then, my youngest would sometimes call and ask when I was coming home. These responsibilities helped me establish my boundaries. Yes, I was a scientist and passionate about my work, but I loved my family, and I would not succumb to the pressure put on women to choose between career and family. I would buck the system and have both.

My success at L'Oréal was both personal and professional. I traveled internationally collecting data, doing research, and conducting studies that would affect global beauty industry standards and practices. I was tasked with leading teams. I contributed to the scientific body of knowledge by publishing in peer-reviewed journals. I was honored with speaking to teams of scientists and industry professionals. Sometimes, I was overwhelmed by the sense of pride exhibited by Black people in other countries who were so proud to see a professional who looked like them. To outsiders, it probably seemed like I was constantly winning or living a charmed professional life, but I can honestly say that everything I accomplished was done under an undercurrent of fear. As a Black, female scientist, I was always proving myself through my research and knowledge. Even in the study of ethnic hair care, there was an imposed hierarchy of knowledge and intelligence based on stereotypes and industry discrimination. This is something that most Black scientists deal with. I resolved within myself to shatter these preconceived notions, never letting them get in the way of my success. I pushed myself to be the best in the industry, take chances, be heard, and uplift the voices of others like myself.

As I mastered my profession, I sensed a change. While I was happy with my research, my truest sense of fulfillment came from helping others. Projects in which my success positively affected someone else's outcome gave me hope and inspiration. I started to rethink whether I was truly using all my skills and talents to their full potential or whether I was falling into the trap of living in the status quo. After careful consideration and planning, I decided that it was time for me to move on.

I left my corporate job and laid out a plan for my own business. People told me it was a mistake. I was leaving a high paying career that afforded me a multitude of benefits along with once-in-a-lifetime global travel experiences to work part-time at a university and grow a business. Yes, I was afraid, but I was also determined. Every doubter increased my desire for success. Every time something didn't go as planned, I worked harder.

Even though every move I made was stepping into the unknown, I stepped with preparation and purpose.

Sometimes you disrupt your career to find it. I set about the task of blending my love of hair science with my desire to serve individuals. It was arduous. And it was frightening. Every aspect of my success depended on my efforts. It was also invigorating. I built a system of research and services that empowered women of color, both as individuals and as entrepreneurs. I spoke at conferences and workshops to stylists and emphasized increasing collaboration, training, and knowledge of ingredients and hair composition. I serviced individual women by performing personalized hair analysis, allowing them to not only advocate for their best hair care but to take care of it on their own.

Along with this, my university work gave me the opportunity to pour my knowledge into underrepresented minority students in science. I helped develop and support programs that created a pipeline for increasing the numbers of minorities in science. I was a listening ear and encourager for students afraid of what being Black in science meant. I shared my challenges and successes and served as an example of what could be if you did things your way.

It was not without sacrifice. Disrupting my career meant that my family dynamic would change. This is where your anchors matter. Anchors provide you stability and hold you in place – they keep you grounded. I married a man that believed in my vision. I had a mother that supported my ideas. I had two daughters that saw me as a role model. I surrounded myself with friends who prayed for my success.

Leaving the corporate world strained the financial stability of our home. With my business and part-time university work, I only made a fraction of my past six-figure salary. I had asked everyone to make sacrifices. At one point, things had gotten so tight that my always supportive husband said he "didn't sign up for this." It wasn't a deal-breaker or a sign of wavering support; it was just a fact. I had to realize that while I was operating in fear, my anchors were also afraid. The best anchors keep you honest. My husband trusted me to be successful, and his willingness to express his own apprehension strengthened my resolve and challenged me to create other avenues to expand my business.

Disruption - radical change to an existing industry or market due to technological innovation.

In the beginning, I don't believe it was my intent to be disruptive. As a student, a mother and an employee, I acted on gut instinct and the intrinsic value of my self-worth and work. It wasn't easy, but I learned to stand up for myself and to maintain my principles in ways that gave me confidence. I learned to sacrifice when necessary and when to step back. Now, I am intentionally disruptive.

Disrupting the hair care industry is my goal.

The hair care industry can be cutthroat. In my business, I've encountered many stylists who are secretive about their work and their clients. Some of this is based on fear—the fear of losing clients, fear of not understanding specific techniques, and fear of understanding product ingredients and how they work. If the industry is to move to the next level, it must do away with business as usual.

My business structure has evolved to help stylists work in an entirely different manner. I am providing education to hair professionals about Black hair that is based on novel research. Using technology, I am helping them elevate their own businesses and services. I ask them to celebrate collaboration instead of competition. My company trains stylists in a format that builds the brand of qualified professionals, giving them specialized training that uses science to take hair care to the next level. I've taken all the information learned in my career and personal research and am sharing it with other individuals.

As the founder of the Our Black Hair Matters Movement, I am a trusted resource for the Black community, hair professionals, and industry leaders who are passionate about supporting healthy hair as it relates to products, services, research, and education.

We saw disruption in the industry as Black women have shifted toward embracing natural hair, as companies began formulating paraben and sulfate-free products, and more ingredients from nature. This is an even bigger disruption. I plan to bring data to the forefront to truly analyze products' efficacy, and safety on Black hair. I want the entire population to understand how Black hair is affected by formulations, environment, lifestyle, and genetics and then champion products that are marketed for Black hair and created for Black hair.

My purpose is to collaborate with stylists, estheticians, trichologists, and other industry leaders to improve the Black hair care industry. The Our Black Hair Matters Movement is meant to empower the entire Black community to make informed decisions about hair and scalp health. If you believe Black hair matters, I invite you to learn more and join the movement at www.OurBlackHairMatters.com.

I've talked about my legacy of disruption in my life, family, career, and industry. But, let me tell you about the ultimate disruption. Disrupting my mentality. The first thing I had to conquer through everything I achieved was my own thoughts and preconceived notions. I had to move beyond negative thinking and keep myself on track despite mistakes, obstacles, and challenges. No matter how hard something seemed, I had to put effort into trying. We know that we can be our own worst enemy. Disrupt that thinking. Be your own best supporter instead.

There will be many times when you are scared. When the thought of starting something new or starting over or admitting you've made a mistake will seem like the point of no return, don't be held hostage by fear. Let it motivate you and guide you. Let the fear fuel your passion, let it increase your stamina, and heighten your awareness. Fear tells us we are doing something uncomfortable, something challenging, but can also signify something monumental. Don't let fear tell you what you can't do. Instead, let it guide you through what you haven't done…yet.

About Crystal E. Porter, Ph.D.

Crystal E. Porter, Ph.D. is a hair scientist and owner of Mane Insights, Inc, a company that conducts research to further understand the specific needs of the hair and scalp. As a recognized contributor in the world of hair science, she also provides knowledge about hair to individuals, professionals and industry leaders. She is passionate about debunking myths and empowering others to properly care for their hair. Her patent-pending process helps individuals tailor their hair care regimen for their own individual needs.

Dr. Porter began her career in cosmetic science at Unilever where she conducted research for aid-to-formulation. She spent the majority of her 20-year career at L'Oréal, USA where she managed the Physics Laboratory and Consumer Insights teams. During the past fifteen years, she has shared knowledge about ethnic hair with fellow scientists at national and global venues. She has also contributed to L'Oréal's global classification of curl in hair and has authored scientific papers, presentations and book chapters on hair straightening and ethnic hair.

ANGELA DELOACH ELLINGTON

Expert Author

Prepared to Pivot:
Moving Forward with Faith and Purpose

By: Angela DeLoach Ellington

I like to think of my life journey as a river's flow. A river often starts small, just a trickle at the base of a mountain.

My journey began as a small idea. As a young girl growing up in Savannah, Georgia, I was blessed to be surrounded by strong role models. Generations of women who showed me the importance of taking care of self and taking care of others. Women whose belief in family and community was evident in how they lived their lives. Growing up, my grandmother often housed and fed those in need. My mother worked in public housing, becoming the first woman to serve as Director of Public Housing in Savannah. I was blessed to have a village of diverse strong women which also included my aunts, sisters, and older female cousins. All of these powerful women poured into me ideals and motivations that would shape my future. I saw and I learned an appreciation for faith, family, and service.

Very slowly the river grows. It begins to take shape; it moves faster, cutting its own path. It flows over rocks, around tree limbs, and slips between the smallest crevice without hesitation.

I was inspired. By the third grade, I knew what my future held. I wanted to become a doctor. My natural curiosity and love of science coupled with a desire to make people feel better made this the perfect choice. I would use my talent to encourage wellness and solve problems. I would listen and learn from the people I served and use my knowledge and resources to provide them with health and longevity tools. This passion stayed with me through my elementary and high school years and I entered Spelman College in pursuit of a BS in Biology, one more step toward my goal.

31

The thing about pursuing a goal is that life is unpredictable. I navigated my way through college, honing my skills in science and research. I earned an opportunity to intern at a state hospital. Since I was planning to become a pediatrician, I was given a position in the neonatal unit. Everything I had worked for was coming to fruition, until I realized that watching newborn babies face death was too overwhelming. As much as I wanted to participate in the joy of birth and to help new parents adjust, the anxiety of loss was not something I wanted to witness frequently. The situation was alarming, and it was clear that I needed to make a change. While I was uncertain of a future without a career in medicine, I was not afraid.

Sometimes, the river hits a bend. An expanse of land rises and prevents its forward movement. The river is not thwarted. It knows its job is to keep moving forward, so it turns and continues to travel.

We are told as children to "dream big". Those dreams always end up related to something tangible; being a doctor, a teacher, or an engineer. When we change those dreams and pivot for an unexpected reason, it is often seen as negative. We think we aren't moving forward or living up to our expectations. We feel as if we are being forced to change, that we are adjusting and surviving instead of growing. I could have believed that not becoming a pediatrician meant my dreams were lost, but I knew I was a caregiver and loved science. I knew that my education and experience held value. I knew my purpose was to help others. I knew that God had given me this purpose and I would move in it with faith. Because I knew my purpose, I was prepared to achieve it by venturing down another path. I decided that I would attend graduate school and pursue a master's in public health.

Sometimes, tributaries feed into the river; bringing knowledge from other lakes, partnering to create power, and opportunities to flow further.

Knowing and following your purpose, exercising patience and persistence is one of the keys to realizing your goals. Another is listening and accepting assistance. This is important as you are on your journey, many will try to pour into you, each one bringing new ideas, new challenges, and new paths. It's up to you to decipher which is right. If you stay true to yourself and your goals, you will know who to let in and when. For me, it was my mother and my fiancé. Along with them, was my faith in God. I drew on the knowledge that my life was ordered and if I listened and remained attentive, God would continue to give me guidance.

These thoughts guided me as I prepared for my wedding and honeymoon. I had faith that when we returned, I would continue to seek and find the ideal career opportunity. God's plan was already in motion. I returned from my honeymoon to an opportunity from a company that was the leading manufacturer of ethnic hair care in the country. I interviewed and was offered a position as a Quality Control Chemist. It was not my original career plan, but it was an opportunity in science. I would test finished consumer products opposed to researching and developing them. In my mind, it was a good job but not a career choice. With the support of my husband and trust in God, I accepted the position.

Sometimes, huge droplets of water break through the river's surface. Too fast and the river swells and floods the bank. It can look chaotic, but the river knows how to expand and still move with grace.

Though it was a small company in size and staff, the research and impact on the ethnic hair market was big. My mission and drive were equally as big because the company's output was monumental. I performed multiple duties that at a larger company, would have been assigned to several departments to include research. As a result, the transition to a Research and Development Chemist was a natural move. I was responsible for developing products for ethnic hair which was the ultimate chance to make people feel better. A healthy hair appearance and attractive hairstyles with ease of maintenance are essential to one's emotional and mental well-being. Even in our youth, we are inundated with messages about our appearance. These messages and judgments often continue through adulthood. My position allowed me the ability to address concerns for many women who looked like me. I was excited about creating products for ethnic hair and filling a gap in the market. Seeing my mother stand and fight against the proliferation of racial stereotypes during my childhood, solidified my interest and care for the needs of ethnic minorities. In a world where one's appearance still influences their acceptance; I was honored to be a part of creating products specifically geared to addressing the manageability of ethnic hair.

Sometimes, part of the river veers off, meanders along the earth, creating a gully. This part is not lost. It remains connected to the river, but it also brings new growth to the ground beneath.

It is amazing how God's plan is often so much larger and far-reaching than our own. Although most chemists at the company were black, there was an undercurrent of inequality in terms of expectations and capabilities. The lack of Black female chemists globally put pressure on me to perform above and beyond what was expected. Issues of inequality ranged from subtle to blatant while working under a leader who was comfortable enough to mention a family connection to a white supremacist organization. I made the choice to focus on science. My thought was, everyone may not accept me as a scientist, but my work would stand on its own.

In my heart, I felt protected by God in my work and position. I stayed focused and remained true to my work, faith and beliefs. When you don't let race and gender inequalities influence or bother you, your quiet resistance and high quality of work may be a source of change.

By staying focused, I was promoted to the Director of Product Development, the first African American woman to hold this position within the company. I followed in my mother's footsteps, I had found a direction that fulfilled my passion for developing products, but there was more. I felt compelled that through spiritual and personal growth, I could reach or influence a nation. This is how God can work in your life. The details may not be as you envision and you may not always fully understand, but if you keep walking in faith, God's plan will become clear. Not only will it become clear, but it can shine bright enough to seed and illuminate the path of others.

Sometimes, the river feeds others – providing support and sustenance while maintaining its progress.

After fourteen years, the company was acquired by the #1 cosmetics manufacturer in the world, L'Oréal. I was once again placed in a position of unexpected change. I had excelled at my previous company, but was uncertain of new expectations or inclusion of diversity. I spent time reflecting on my past and knew that I would adapt regardless of the changes and challenges.

My immediate responsibilities remained in ethnic product development. However, the size and dynamics of my team changed drastically along with the level of resources and tools at my disposal. My drive, determination, and research granted me numerous patents, both domestic and international. I became the first African American woman to serve as Assistant Vice President of Research and Innovation for Ethnic Hair Care and Styling. I was charged with interacting and influencing a global team of scientists. I shared ideas, experience, and knowledge in an environment centered on learning. Spiritual and personal awareness led me to know that God was using this position to prepare me for the world's stage. I educated and trained scientists in multiple countries. I became well versed, not only in ethnic haircare, but also developed a deep understanding of research and innovation for all textures of hair. My eight-year-old self could not have imagined me holding this position, but thinking back she had planted the seeds for me through an idea, determination, adaptability and faith. At the time, I thought this was the position I would retire from.

Sometimes, there are rapids – rocks and boulders, dips and waterfalls, waves that rise to seemingly insurmountable heights, but the river forges ahead.

Then I was faced with the biggest obstacle of my life. My husband and confidant for nearly 26 years was diagnosed with cancer. After a short battle, he passed away. On top of that, both of my children were soon to be away at college. It felt like the bottom dropped out of my entire world. A year later, the company I thought had fulfilled my dreams made a business decision to relocate Ethnic Research & Innovation from Chicago to New Jersey. I was faced with moving to a new city without a support system, when I felt the most alone.

During this time, my faith was my sustenance. I relied on God's love and strength to guide me each day. As a person identified as a caregiver and one who is fully committed to establishing, obtaining, and maintaining company goals, it felt like I had reached the end. I had lost my helpmate, I thought I reached a pinnacle in my career and it was all crashing down.

I once again reflected on God's purpose for my life. I looked back on my journey, the ways I was able to change course and find the right footing. I sat still and listened. It was then that I realized the end of my journey was not at L'Oréal. It wasn't just influencing or reaching a global team of scientists, marketers and educators, nor was it about breaking race and gender barriers in corporate appointments. Everything that I learned, experienced, and overcome was preparing me for a new beginning.

Finally, the river reaches the ocean – vast and full of possibilities.

I left the corporate world behind, an end to one phase of my journey, but the beginning of a new life. This new life takes all the years I worked, all the struggles and adversity I've overcome, all the research and tools I've used, all the knowledge that I've acquired, and all the grief and disappointment I've experienced, and puts them to work for a life destined for wholeness and success.

I often reflect on that one idea of making people feel better. I remember how important it was to me then and I know how important it is to me now. Holding strong to this idea and being faithful to God and my purpose led me to establish my own companies. Through them, I can independently pursue what is most important to me. At RTG Research Laboratories LLC, I manufacture Moistura Silk, a haircare brand focused on hair health. My goal is to empower consumers with healthy styling options that look and feel good to them. I also inspire and mentor young women in STEM interested in pursuing a career in the hair care industry. Through D&E Industries, I provide product development and consulting services to cosmetologists, trichologists, beauty entrepreneurs, contract manufacturers, and cosmetic manufacturers. With my help, small, minority entrepreneurs can create and launch their own product lines. My goal with both companies is two-fold: to continue creating and providing high-quality products that promote healthy hair among all communities and to empower young women and men to set and achieve their own goals. This is the manifestation of God's plan.

The ocean is limitless.

It's okay to dream big, but also learn to dream without limits. Be so certain in your purpose that you follow it through every twist and turn. Be so steadfast in your faith that you know God's plan will be reflected in your journey. All you need is one small trickle, the tiniest spark to light your path. For me, it was the idea of making others feel better. That one small motivation led me on a path that curved, dipped, looped, and almost veered off course, but ultimately brought me to a new beginning. I am now walking in my destiny, my purpose; a place of help and a place of hope. Whatever lies ahead, I am prepared to continue moving forward with faith and purpose.

To learn more about Angela D. Ellington's companies, visit us at www.deindustriesinc.com and www.moisturasilk.com. To schedule speaking engagements or interviews, contact me at aellington@deindustriesinc.com.

About Angela DeLoach Ellington

Angela DeLoach Ellington, scientist, inventor and industry expert in the field of ethnic research and innovation is the founder and chief executive officer of D&E Industries Inc. and Moistura Silk. Angela's career spans nearly three decades of driving business success for global personal care companies by leading the development of innovative products for textured hair. She is recognized as an authority in the field of product development. As an authority in the field, she has authored and co-authored a body of work in the cosmetic industry and has been awarded several patents in the field of hair care research. Angela is the former Assistant Vice President of Ethnic Research and Innovation at L'Oréal USA. Under her leadership, she championed and inspired ethnic research and innovation for the conglomerate's North America, Europe, Brazil and Africa operations. In her new role, she will continue to focus on the uniqueness of ethnic product development as well as inspire and mentor STEM major students interested in the field of cosmetic science. Ms. Ellington received a Bachelor of Science degree in biology from Spelman College.

DEON JOHNSON

Who Do You Think You Are?

By: Deon Johnson

If you're black, brown, female, gay, been abused, been marginalized, or simply forgotten, and you're struggling to turn your side hustle into a thriving business endeavor, I have knowledge for you to change the game TODAY! You might be someone who has started an endeavor and is struggling or you maybe someone who needs a little push to get off the sideline and into the game. I got you. My sole purpose with my career and my reason for writing this chapter is to be a resource to people like you — the minority entrepreneur. You have been unserved and undervalued, but you already have what I believe is the very thing that will make you successful. But before we go any further together, I need you to understand and accept two things.

1. No matter how big your vision is, and no matter how much you've done (or haven't done), you're closer than you think.

2. You will accomplish your vision because of some things you have already experienced in life. And you don't need to learn anything new. Yo! You already got it!

If you're wanting to be a business owner, if you're wishing to get your side hustle off the ground or planning to take that side hustle it to the next level or if you're seeking a better life, shit is going to happen to you. Trust me — knockdowns and setbacks are, for sure, coming your way. To me the setbacks and knockdowns are only the universe questioning your commitment to achieving these goals. How you handle these seemingly destructive obstacles is key.

I started by rattling off race, sexual orientation, sex and certain life traumas because those conditions and happenings make you a minority in this country, and we minorities in America are given a gift — you just have

41

to choose to see it that way. The gift you've been given is your tribulations and your afflictions. Stay with me. Pretend for a minute that all the trials you've ever experienced are placed neatly in a box and tied up with a pretty bow and left on your doorstep. No matter how difficult it may seem, I want you to choose to see all that rough stuff you've been through this way. Because they are gifts.

It's important to note, too, that you do not have to learn anything new to accomplish your dreams. You may not know it, but you already have what it takes. Let that sink in — know you're set to get started today, whether you feel it or not.

"He who says he can and he who says he can't are both usually right."- Confucius

Now, let me tell you a story that answers one of my favorite questions, "Who do you think you are?" Be careful though...

I grew up a poor black boy in broken and broke homes, which presented ample challenges and insecurities for me. Those insecurities often controlled my thinking and influenced my behavior to sway toward the unhealthy. They convinced me to believe the lies and sabotaged any drive to break free from where I was. In short, they dominated my value system and how I viewed life and most importantly, how I viewed myself. I'm a dreamer by nature, so often I've had dope visions, fire ideas and game-changing concepts, but I had people in my life who thought my lack of formal education and experience made me unworthy of bringing any of these things to fruition.

Those infiltrations into my own self-worth and confidence became shackles wrapped around ankles, and once again I had to ask myself, "Who do you think you are?" Because of the way I grew up, my first answers to that question weren't any good at all, so the shackles stayed locked on and got heavier, remained and came with me.

Growing up, there were times my family couldn't even pay the utility bill. There were times my family didn't even have furniture. My mom was always robbing Peter to pay Paul, and yet still coming up short. There was never enough. And the prevailing thought was that there will never be enough. It is as if those moments were asking me instead, "Who are you to think you can succeed?" and making me feel as though I was destined to fail. Or even worse, never start.

I lost years of universal and simple production because I bought into what those embarrassing moments were telling me: "You are not enough." They were also always saying, "How can you possibly accomplish your big dream from where you came from?" I could not answer that question for a very long time. What I wish I had done was seen all those burdens neatly wrapped up in that pretty packaging we talked about. I wish I could have seen them as a gift earlier, because I wasted time only seeing them as obstacles.

"Where you are almost doesn't matter, it's where you're headed that matters most."- Lerna Scott

So, we've covered who I thought I was when I was failing, now let's get to the good stuff. To do that, I have to go back to my very beginning. October 10, 1970 changed the world! It was the day the world was introduced to Deon Charles Johnson, and it will never be the same for sure, because of what I hope to share with you. I am named after Dionne Warrick and my great grandfather on my dad's side while carrying my pop's last name. I am very much my brother's keeper to Jabbar. I am also the textbook mama's boy to the one that gave me my eternal never dying hope, Lerna Scott, my only superhero.

I am an entrepreneur because I am a minority. I am a minority because I am an entrepreneur. To me, they truly are one in the same. If you are reading this, and you are a minority, don't get it twisted. You are already an entrepreneur. Simply put, the definition of an entrepreneur is one that manages risk. I can't think of anyone who manages risk better and more than a minority. It's really all we know.

How did I so quickly change my answer to "Who do you think you are?" I owe it to the year 2010.

A decade ago, I'm in my place of business carrying out the day to day. A realization hit me so hard I almost passed out, so it's a moment I can't forget. I had been working my tail off in my first startup.

In the fall of 2008, I started my first fitness center. It was and remains my baby. I personally raised the capital, I personally negotiated the terms of the lease, I personally oversaw the buildout, and I personally prepared a team for a successful and fruitful venture. There was only one small hiccup ... I started my company during the worst U.S. economy since The Great Depression. Things were much harder than anticipated and needless to say, we suffered mightily and quickly. Revenue was slow yet the landlord wanted theirs, AT&T wanted theirs, Reliant Energy wanted theirs. Everybody wanted theirs. Not to mention my investors wanted thiers. And I didnt have any of theirs. I did not think I was going to make it. Instead of giving up, I created a plan, I prayed and kept showing up to work as if we were a healthy, robust company. The plan, prayer and work paid off. We were able to turn things around rather quickly and get everyone theirs to keep our doors open and my dream alive.

"When you want to succeed as bad as you want to breathe, then you'll be successful."- ET

What changed for us? In that time frame, in struggling to right our ship, I didn't get any smarter. I didn't get any better. I didn't get any more money. Without realizing it at the time, I was applying the lessons learned by enduring those hard times of growing up poor, listening to voices telling me I wasn't good enough and of suffering through embarrassment time and time again.

Now, back to that magnificent and powerful moment in 2010. The veracity of the realization was so much that I finally understood I was viewing and thinking of entrepreneurship and business altogether in the wrong light. I had it all wrong until that moment. Before that, I thought a business was successful because the owner was more educated than me, had more money than me, knew more than me and was just predestined to be more successful. I never stopped to think that he was being asked that same question but had a different answer.

Like most minorities, I grew up not having. I grew up with a strong desire to have what "the others" had. And, as mentioned, I suffered through many embarrassing moments. Growing up my family constantly moved from apartment complex to apartment complex because of cash flow issues. I remember a place we lived that my friends couldn't come over, because we had no living or dining room furniture. There were some nights we were forced to live by candlelight as a family because we couldn't afford to break off the necessary bread for the utility company to keep the lights on. What I realize now is that all of those struggles were gifts from God. I just couldn't see it back then.

Now I understand the value of the embarrassing moments in my childhood, and I'm here to say to minorities who aspire to own their own business, schedules and future: you already have what it takes. The only reason I turned my first startup around and was able to go on to found and start up other companies and thrive as a business consultant is because of my experiences growing up that formed within me a resilience that one cannot just be born with. I have accomplished a few things I couldn't have without enduring those moments. I have helped to lead numerous minority owned startups successfully move through concept to operating to growth and then expansion. I'm proud to tell you I have produced a TV show that highlights healthy living. I am also currently working on another startup I can't wait to share with the world. But most importantly, I know I am in the sweet spot of where I've always wanted to be — telling my story to those who look like me and helping those that look like me. Those moments of yesterday prepared me for the success my business sees today. They gave me the ability to handle setbacks and provided the realization that change and obstacles are inevitable. It's what you do with them that matters most. In short, they were teaching me the valuable lesson of staying in the fight and never surrendering to those feelings of inadequacy until I was able to answer that question differently. And finally win.

"No matter how bad it is or how it gets ... I'm going to make it."-
Les Brown

What I've found is that your ability to navigate through rough waters and stay positive when your revenue is negative or everything and everyone is telling you or even begging you to stop is the only reason people are successful in business. Period. From Fortune 500 companies to side hustles it's the ability to handle setbacks and stay in the game. Don't be fooled. And here's the thing, as a minority you already have that going for you. Your foreseeable success can be derived from the simple fact of what you've survived before. You just have to open that box with the pretty bow at your doorstep and get your gift. After all, you're still standing here today, aren't you? Reading this book, hoping to improve your life and looking to do major things. That alone shows that you've already overcome at least some of the voices telling you you're not good enough and you can't make it. Now it's time to answer the other voices so we can claim what is rightfully yours because of the price you've already paid. You made it past those embarrassing moments! Make it count TODAY and NOW.

It's actually very similar to a boxing event. Typically, the winning gladiator usually is the one who takes the most punches until he lands his knockout punch. In business, the successful owner is not always the most educated or experienced or even the most funded. More often than you may want to believe, it is the one who can endure the most loss and take the most blows until they find that little sliver of hope and opportunity of revenue to complete their vision. If you're a minority, life has thrown a great amount of punches your way, and you are still standing. As a minority, your embarrassing moments and all the punches life has thrown at you and more importantly how you've already overcome them is what makes you different from "them" and are what will empower you to achieve your dream. You just have to believe! These moments in yesterday may have had you feeling some type of way, but today you should rejoice and make the choice to see them as the building blocks that made you strong, resilient, experienced and has given you lessons to learn how to overcome anything. And the defining reason that makes you successful.

The only reason I moved from operating a shaky first startup to where I am today is because of what those moments taught me — keep going. That key principle is everything, and those embarrassing moments gave me a gift. All those moments made me tougher, made me trust myself, forced me to learn, and ultimately filled in the gaps in my life of the things I didn't have — education, money, people, confidence. If you're a minority they're trying to do the same for you. Let them…

"Greatness is not some wonderful, esoteric, god-like feature that only the special among us will taste, it's something that truly exists in all of us." - Will Smith

Let's be crystal clear. As a minority you already have what it takes to be a successful entrepreneur. God has already given you the number one trait you have to have to be successful in business — resilience. The ability to get back up after you've been knocked down. Earlier I mentioned conditions or happenings that make you a minority in this country. I also shared embarrassing moments of mine that you might relate to because peeps like you and me have always had to manage life by juggling between affliction and effect. The affliction is what happened to us and the effect is what we do about it. Clarity comes when we view the embarrassing moments through the proper lenses of them being precious yet powerful. We took them. We got past them. And somehow deep down inside we know we are made whole through them. I want you to acknowledge them, accept them, recount the lessons learned from them, and know you will succeed beyond your wildest dreams because of them — "and for some, in spite of them." The question now is "What do you do with this information?" You

47

can keep doing what you've always done and get what you've always received or you can take the same powerful information and tell a different story that leads you to a different outcome — where you were always destined to be. Keep going — you have already gone through the hardest part of accomplishing your vision. In addition to the two things I asked you to understand and accept at the front of our talk, I want you to also understand that those experiences as a minority are the reason you are stronger today, and what has prepared you for success as an entrepreneur. Now, let's go get knocked down again and again and again. Always getting back up knowing those things that knock us down are only here to help us succeed beyond our wildest dreams. But most importantly, when life or your vision asks you the question "Who do you think you are" you will stand up and proudly answer the way I did after I finally accepted my new identity. And you will say "Enough."

Thank God, and thank you.

"To live is to suffer. To survive, well that's to find meaning in the suffering..."- DMX

Your Invitation

When I work with entrepreneurs I try my best to do three things for them: I work to educate, I want to support, and I mean to challenge. It is my sincere hope that this chapter has achieved the first two: educate and support. Now I wish to make my mark with the last one, challenge. Many minorities who long for their own business and have what it takes don't even make it to the starting block simply because of not having access to the capital they "think" they need. They don't start acting on their dream simply because they feel getting the dough is the hardest thing and will be the reason they can't move forward. I'm here to tell you, as a minority entrepreneur, getting the dough is the easiest part of the game. In fact, just contact me with your elevator pitch, and I will get your project funded for you. No games. No gimmicks. No hooks.

Keeping it 1000. It's nice to be published. It's nice for people to read my words. But please know the one thing I hold above all is influence. I want to be of value to anyone wanting to take their game to the next level! After reading this, if you have questions about this narrative, if you wish to discuss what's next for you, or if you simply want to brainstorm together to outline possibilities and opportunities, I'm down like four flats and I'm here to ensure your success by proving based on your enduring embarrassing moments as a minority that you're already ready. Please get at me TODAY. Let's get your vision popping and jumping together … you and me.

deon@theonefitness.com
713.409.4300

FIVE LAWS TO KEEP MINORITY ENTREPRENEURS TO STAY IN THEIR LANE

1. Hold what you got until you get what you need...

   In the beginning, focus on the small victories.

2. Play chess not checkers...

   Every decision affects all decisions.

3. Always be hungry. Never be thirsty...

   Respect yourself. Respect your value. Respect your pricing.

4. It's a minor setback for a major comeback...

   You're going to get knocked down — simply get back up knowing things will get better.

5. You have to work at least twice as hard as non-minority entrepreneurs...

   You know why.

About Deon Johnson

Nutrition expert and personal trainer Deon Johnson has spent more than a decade inspiring men and women to reach their personal health and fitness goals. His passion to see people get healthy, coupled with his sound reputation, has made him a respected professional in the field.

As the owner and founder of The ONE Fitness in Houston, Deon empowers his clients mentally and spiritually to work hard to achieve what they want out of life. The ONE Fitness teaches clients that weight loss is more about knowledge than pure will power, so education is part of everyone's total-health program.

"Helping someone lose weight is easy," Deon said. "Changing the way they live is difficult, but that's my goal."

Deon's philosophy is "Keep It Simple," a belief that helps inspire his clients to remain focused on their own optimal health through the ups and downs of their normal experiences. His clients adhere to the mantra that a steady routine with weight and cardio training helps them get into shape and feel better about themselves.

"Life inevitably causes stress," Deon said. "Stress leads to other health issues. My goal is to keep my clients focused on the things they can do to stay healthy so they can handle anything life throws their way."

"When Deon comes into your life, things are bound to change for the better," said one client. "When I started with Deon, he helped me strengthen my muscles, run faster, lean up and clean up my diet. Now I feel great!"

Deon has trained in the most prestigious facilities in the country, but The ONE Fitness was his longtime dream. The unique health and fitness club is more than a company ... it's a life-changing journey that leads you to a new level of personal growth. An added benefit is the on-premise availability of massages, facials and delicious meals.

Deon has achieved national certifications in all areas that directly influence the success of his clients, including licensing from the **National**

Academy of Sports Medicine (resistance training), **Apex Nutrition** (nutrition and supplements education) and **Keiser Power Pacing Program** (aerobic training). The longtime personal trainer keeps up with the most recent practices and standards by attending the latest training workshops, classes and seminars throughout the country.

A sought-after speaker and presenter, he has been featured on local radio and television talk shows and was the resident fitness expert for KIAH-Channel 39's "Outlook Houston." He also hosts a talk show on local cable network Houston Media Source, where topics have included "Healthy Cooking at Home" and "Tracking Your Weight Loss."

The ONE Fitness is about teaching a lifestyle, and by creating his vision, Deon changes the lives of those who trust him to work alongside them to make that happen.

Learn more about Deon Johnson and The ONE Fitness by visiting www.theonefitness.com.

ARNETTA L. ROGERS

Like Butter, Her Cup Runneth Over!

By: Arnetta L. Rogers

I was poppin! The year was 1990; I had my own apartment, my own government job, my own car, and no children. It's when you least expect it that certain encounters come to change your life. It was a beautiful summer night when one of my best friends and I was invited to a party. Feeling good, we went to the party, and before I could step both feet in the yard where the party was, someone grabbed my hand. Startled, I jerked away and eased my way to the lady's room. After using the ladies' room, I opened the door and to my surprise, the same guy who had grabbed my hand was at the door of the lady's room. Now at this point, I'm really thinking he's a creep, but to my surprise, I knew his sister through a cousin of mine. He quickly asked his sister to tell me he was cool, and she did. After that, we danced and ended up talking on the front porch of the house, which turned out to be his Moms' house and a birthday party for him. At the time, I was on the tail end of a relationship with a guy I'd met in high school. My new guy was handsome, charming, older, had no children, and protective; overly protective! He knew exactly what to do! He started paying my rent, buying me things, taking me to nice places, and he could sing. Ladies, what more can you ask for at 20? A year later, we married in August 1992. He was 31, I was 21, and we were happy. In May of 1993, we had our first child, a beautiful daughter, and 22 months later, we had our second child, a handsome son. We bought a home together; we both had successful careers and began a life together. Life was good, except my older husband wanted more of my time—the time I spent on my new career as a cosmetologist. He began to do things that were destructive to the marriage to get my attention. I respected his role, but it seemed he didn't respect mine. Because of my outgoing nature, it became clear that what looked like protection before became a problem. I thought he was controlling, over-protective, and unreasonable. He thought I was naïve, young, and stupid. He began to cheat, and before long, the other woman made it clear she was in the picture. Over time his verbal and mental abuse had gotten worse; it started to wear me down. Unfortunately, the children never really

55

got to see how happy we were because they were both so young when we started having problems.

They say, where there is darkness, God will send light. One spring evening, I decided to go out with the family to a local club. Anyone who knows my family knows that we love to have fun together. Well, on this particular day, I felt good, looked good and was ready to enjoy myself. Sitting at a booth with my cousins in the club, looking down at my drink, well, let's just call him a "cleverly disguised distraction." This cleverly disguised distraction came and would again change the trajectory of my life. It was an instant feeling I had never felt before. He asked me to dance; I was shocked because number one, I was married and thought the world knew it, and two, because I instantly became insecure. Insecure, because at the time, I thought I was a tough cookie you know, fighting mental and verbal abuse and standing up for myself through it all. What I didn't realize is that I was broken. And what I now call my cleverly disguised distraction turned out to be just what I needed to get through, so I thought. This distraction became my confidant; he didn't hurt me and listened intently. He was super attractive, and our chemistry was off the charts! Whew! I swear neither he nor I knew what to do with this newfound energy. Let's face it, I was married, and he had someone who would later become his wife. Although physically, we were true to our relationships, we began an emotional affair that lasted longer than we both care to admit. My husband found out, and of course, his behavior worsened, and we ended up in a very bitter custody battle that lasted for years. I was in the tug of war of my life! I was determined not to let this man solely raise my children. But my cleverly disguised distraction always knew what to say and when to say it. I hung on to his every word as if my life depended on it! As time went on, my husband's affair continued, and so did my emotional affair. We separated in 1997 but still couldn't get along, sadly, not even for the children.

I moved out of the house and started my healing process. It was a relief to be out of such a toxic space. Still having regular conversations with my distraction, I had become co-dependent. We both had, which wasn't good for either of us. One summer evening, while talking in his car, he asked me if I was going back to my husband. Well, ladies, even through all I had gone through, I told this man yes. I had to give it one last shot for my children. My mouth said yes, but my heart was screaming nooo! But what he didn't tell me was that his then-girlfriend had become pregnant and he would marry her. Four months had gone by, and now I knew for sure the decision to leave my ex-husband was the right one. But oops, wait a minute! My cleverly disguised distraction had gotten married, and I knew nothing about it. Another month had passed, and I couldn't stop thinking about him. Candidly having a conversation with a local celebrity DJ, who has since passed on, God rest his soul; he told me that he'd just Deejayed his wedding. Not only did my heart drop, but it also stopped! Lol I pulled out my Rolodex, called a buddy in his inner circle, and he confirmed. I still couldn't believe it; I had to find out from the horse's mouth! I knew where he worked, so I called the directory with the help of a friend, and they connected me to his office. I have to admit, when I heard his voice, it sounded like music to my ears. I could see his smile through the phone. We laughed and talked for a bit, and then I had to ask him what seemed like the hardest question of my life. Are you Married? Did you get married? He didn't answer right off. He said we needed to talk and asked what I would be doing that weekend? Of course, whatever plans I had had to be put on hold. Lol. I flew to Chicago, which was the first time I'd heard the Honorable Minister Louis Farrakhan speak. He had been studying the teachings of the Honorable Elijah Muhammad; peace be upon him, which explains why he was so good with me. While in Chicago, he told me he had gotten married. I was devastated! I cried my eyes out in Chicago, but he still handled me with care. I have to admit it took me some time because I had grown so dependent on his council and our friendship. It was a painful process, but I knew I had to let go. A couple of years had gone by as the year 2000 rolled in, I could genuinely laugh and not feel pretentious. I had custody of my children, and by now, I'd even gone on a couple of dates. Admittedly, still having regular communication with my distraction, and as a new member of the Nation of Islam, I began to discover my strength in my faith while struggling to let go of a friendship I knew had to end. I began to study and pray. During my studies, while reading my study guides, one in particular resonated with me. "Rising above your emotions into the thinking of God" was not only my favorite, but it was what I needed. I read it over and over again! I know and use this lesson in my life today. Talk about a tug of war! Whew! It got me through! As a Muslim girl in training (MGT) learning the seven units from the Honorable Elijah Muhammad's teachings, you learn how to structure your life to be suited for God and a husband.

Prayer most definitely works! It was October 2000; my prayers were answered. I'd prayed for a husband. I no longer wanted to be single, and I certainly didn't want to be codependent on a married man. I prayed for a man with a heart like mine who loved me past my faults and me the same. I was very specific in my prayer down to some very personal things, and I tell you, God answered big time! After twelve years of being away, my childhood sweetheart came looking for me. He came with a job and an open heart and was fine as wine! Ladies, you know how they look when they first come home...Lol A mutual friend had given him my work number, and he called. I missed the call, and he left a message. I have to admit, when I heard the message, I was stuck. I didn't know if I should call or not so I didn't for two weeks. Two weeks had gone by, and I was home alone with no children, all dressed up with nowhere to go, so I called him. He asked me to come over; I said no. He put his mother and his brother on the phone and convinced me to come. I'm so glad I did! I saw the family, and when his brother saw me, he told me his brother had asked about me as soon as he was in town. He said to him, "man! I haven't seen you in years. I am not thinking about Arnetta." But to his surprise, there I was, standing in the living room of their Mom's house. He looked at his brother and said, "damn, man, you weren't playing!" We had a good laugh. That night we left his Mom's house to go for a ride. When he got in my truck, something came over me, and I remembered my prayer. Silently, I asked God was it him? And to my surprise, my new husband-to-be answered yes, looked up at me, and answered yes again with a smile. I was stunned! It was so crystal clear I couldn't deny it. I thought to myself, how did he hear me? Am I crazy? All I could do was smile and drive. We drove around half the night talking. From then on, we were inseparable. I was honest with him about my "cleverly disguised distraction," and all that was going on in my life. He knew what he wanted and told me that he loved me ever since we were children and never stopped. He told me that he was here and that my distraction was not. So, what else could I say to that, ladies? And although he had studied Islam before, it was of a different denomination. He started attending the Mosque with me, and we began to court. While still dealing with the remnants of my first marriage and having my distraction in my rear-view, tragedy struck my family in 2001. On July 21st, 2001, I lost my Mom. Three days after we buried my Mom, my divorce became final in a bitter court hearing. One month later, our family lost one of our beautiful young cousins, only seven years old, and just when we thought it couldn't get any worse, we were hit with yet another blow that would break the hearts of our family to the core. We lost my aunt, my mother's sister, in the Pentagon on 9/11. At this point, I'm truly thinking that the world is coming to an end. My entire family was in shambles! We had just lost a child and two significant pillars in our family that were full of strength, class, guidance and everything that we all needed was gone within two months. It was unimaginable! I had to gird up my loins and fight! Spiritually fight!

I asked God to change my heart, and with time, he did. I told my distraction I was getting married, and he asked me if I was sure. I told him I couldn't wait on him forever, and I married my childhood sweetheart in 2002. Less than a year later, I sold the home I'd purchased after my separation, and my new husband and I purchased my mother's home. It was tough, but every time I wanted to give up, I would hear my mother say, "Don't they know you're unstoppable?!" Something she'd said to me when I was going through tough times. And so, I would keep going.... yeees, Buttercup, we affectionately called her, although her legal name was Ruth. Buttercup had the kind of love that made everyone feel like they were the only one. To know her was to love her. When she passed, at her funeral, even the little children cried. Many still share stories of her love, and it warms my heart every time. At age 31, I had to face life head-on without my Mom. Even when my cup was running over, I would find solace in knowing she equipped me with what I needed. I'd made up my mind to get all the pieces of my life in order. Well, yawl know what happens when you decide to follow the road less traveled, the devil comes every which way

59

but loose! I lost money from a major investment, and we lost my mother's house during the housing crisis.

Once again, I was devastated! Feeling ashamed and completely defeated, in 2007, we decided to move to Charlotte, N.C. It was time to rebuild. We could do what we needed to do in peace. It would be a year before my husband could join us in Charlotte, but he would send his paycheck bi-weekly to take care of us. When my husband finally found a job in Charlotte, he had to take a pay cut, but he quickly rose to the top in skills and pay. We focused on saving, working on our debt, and raising our children. We were on a mission! I eventually opened a salon, sold it, and bought another one before moving back home. I was grinding okay! I worked my salon front in NC and traveled the interstate bi-weekly to my salon suites in Maryland to service my faithful clientele. However, driving every two weeks from Charlotte to the DMV after seven years started to take its toll. While I rented suites to other stylists, I was focused on building my brand beyond before. It was then I realized I had to come from behind the chair to fully dedicate myself to my new venture. I became unstoppable, just like my mother said.

My care for other beauty professionals became my focus, and my motto became "Beauty Entrepreneurs, We Care!" It was no longer about how much we can make in a week but how to become financially secure in a lifetime. Using my experience of over 20 plus years in the industry and the system I'd created for myself; I began to access the resources needed for longevity in health, wellness, and financial security. I developed a system specifically designed for beauty entrepreneurs, which can also be used for small businesses. I created My BMF Solutions, LLC, and partnered with a major software company, ProSolutions Software, to help beauty professionals manage their business. This salon software is not your typical software. It was developed to help beauty professionals and self-employed individuals learn how to manage properly, operate a legitimate business, and pay for health and life insurance all in one system. With its excellent reports, you'd never have to worry about avoiding filing taxes again. I became an Insurance Producer currently licensed in multiple states to provide healthcare, life/business policies and strategies to beauty professionals and many others. Having obtained my Masters' Degree in Professional Cosmetology from The National Beauty Culturists' League, the oldest institute for beauty professionals at 101 years old to date; my system is now mandated as part of its curriculum. I am currently an Instructor with The Institute and in its Doctorate program.

Looking back at the lowest point in my life and now being "In Command"! Hence the book title; I feel truly blessed! My husband and I of almost 19 years come from a place where many don't come out alive, Southeast DC. With God's grace, we managed to survive and have a little fun while doing so, and we are forever grateful!

You may contact me for lectures, business consulting, online courses, my management system, wellness products and more @ IamArnettaRogers.org, mybmfsolutions.network, or email mybmfsolutions@gmail.com. Thank you, and I pray that my story will help you stay the course and become unstoppable in life and in love!

About Arnetta L. Rogers

A beauty industry innovator and visionary with a passion for leading beauty and barber entrepreneurs in business management, medical and financial solutions for building multi-generational wealth. Arnetta is a licensed cosmetologist and beauty entrepreneur with over 25-years in the industry. She is also a licensed life, accident and health Insurance Producer with National Agents Alliance. By coupling her beauty industry experience and resources with her life and financial planning knowledge, Arnetta has created a total professional and personal management solution for today's beauty and barber entrepreneurs. Through My BMF Solutions, Arnetta is committed to bridging the gap between business, personal life, wellness, and longevity in the beauty industry. She is a proud member of the prestigious National Beauty Culturists League with a Masters 2 Professional Cosmetology Degree; a partner with ProSolutions Salon Software; and Board of Directors Member with MI Mother's Keeper, helping to build capital and resources for those who are mentally intelligent and in need of treatment, case management, and community resources. Arnetta has an innate ability to educate, motivate,and guide beauty industry entrepreneurs to achieve, grow, and build both professionally and personally. After working in the industry for a number of years, Arnetta knows sharing the My BMF Solutions Program will provide self employed professionals the tools needed to build success.

BEVERLY COLEMAN

The Tear That Never Dropped

By: Beverly Coleman

My story begins in North Gulfport, Mississippi, with Dorothy "Dot" Coleman. We couldn't call her "Mom" or "Mother," but after a couple of smacks for not calling her "Dot," we stopped asking questions. Dot, my siblings—Billy, Patricia, Israel, Alfred—and I lived in one bedroom in an old schoolhouse. The limited food helped a mother and her five children squeeze into the two twin beds at the back of the room. When I pass by the Isiah Fredrick Community Center, I'm reminded of the one-bedroom schoolhouse that stood in its place.

Every Sunday, we attended Greater Mt. Olive Baptist Church on Tennessee Ave. While Dot was chastising Alfred for talking during the service, I was busy praying for The Lord to change our situation. God heard my prayers because we moved to a house on West Railroad Ave. It needed work, but at least it had three bedrooms. More space meant more cleaning. Soon it also meant another baby brother, Patrick. Even though the food was scarce with a sixth child, it was always delicious.

We were raised like little soldiers with tough love and no support for achievements. Every Saturday morning at 7 a.m., we would dust, mop, do laundry, cut the grass, pick the fallen pecans and the figs from the tree in our yard. Dot would always tell us, "I had children to do chores and take care of the house." My grandfather was our saving grace on early Saturday mornings. He used to tell Dot to ease up on us. It was like talking to a brick wall. Dot was fifteen years old when she married her twenty-one-year-old husband. The abuse she experienced manifested in her anger toward her children. Dot grabbed whatever she could for discipline: a switch, a belt; she even cut the cord to a steam iron once. You either obeyed her or received physical punishment. I never shed a tear because she taught me at a young age to never show weakness.

When I was nine years old, Dot would send me to borrow cooking ingredients. I hated going to the grey house because the dirty old man was always there alone. He liked to use his slow, sticky fingers to be handsy with little girls, so I started moving quickly. I was afraid to tell an adult. Instead, I told my friend, Darlene, about the battles I faced in the grey house; she wanted to fight too. From then on, Darlene always went to the grey house with me.

That next year Mississippi faced Category 5 Hurricane Camille. We huddled, terrified in my grandfather's house. When my grandfather brought us home, I saw that the grey house was leveled. That was the happiest day of my childhood: I never had to run or fight in that grey house ever again.

When Dot had her seventh child, my sister Ruth, she seemed to love this baby a little more than the rest of us. I was just happy for some joy in the house. Dot's love for Ruth made room for me to explore the game of basketball. My oldest brother Joe Kidd used to say, "I put you on my team to pass and dribble the ball only." He was a trash talker and a standout athlete. Joe is where most of my skills came from; he was setting me up for greatness.

I loved basketball. Basketball didn't scream at or abuse me. It wasn't whipping me for someone else's mistakes or for wrongly carving a chicken. It wasn't hitting my knuckles with a wooden ruler for an incorrect math problem or calling me "big lips" or "skinny legs." I put all of my frustrations and disappointments and hopes and dreams into mastering the game of basketball. I never shed any tears, though; they were a sign of weakness.

Once, when I was about ten years old, Dot and I went to Mr. Charlie May's grocery store. They were white owners in a black neighborhood. We were waiting to check out when Ms. Ann, a white woman, spoke to my mother. She said, "Gal, get my bags for me." I was shaking; I knew what was coming next. Ms. Ann repeated herself, and Dot slapped her down to the floor. We left the groceries and sprinted home. Years passed before we returned to Mr. Charlie's store. We were the original "The Color Purple"!

At twelve years old, Dot put me in charge of cooking for the house and managing my three younger siblings. I matured overnight: I knew how Dot reacted when things weren't perfect. Even the neighborhood kids lived in

66

fear of Dot's rules. They spent the afternoons playing in our backyard, but they scattered like rats when the lookout person saw Dot walking home. They knew she didn't allow visitors while she was gone. Even at a distance, she maintained control.

In high school, my friends talked on the phone and hung out with each other. Dot wasn't having that, and I was too afraid to ask for permission. All I could do was master basketball as a Point Guard. At home, I was nobody; but I was the world's greatest entertainer on the court. I would practice in stormy weather and pretend that the raindrops were my screaming fans. Dot allowed me to play, but it was short-lived. Dot never learned to drive, so we walked many places until Dot asked my Uncle Johnnie to teach me to drive. Afterward, driving Dot was my newest responsibility.

My outlook changed when I joined the Harrison Central High School girls' basketball program. Under the leadership of Sports Hall of Fame Head Coach Van Chancellor, our 1976-1978 girls basketball season record was 80 wins and 6 losses. By senior year, the college scouts never missed a game. At least 30 different colleges asked me to visit, but my life took an unexpected turn: Greg, a neighborhood boy, liked me. I wasn't allowed to date under Dot's roof, so we started sneaking around. We spent time together at school and on the basketball court. Before Greg, I was set to play college basketball; then, I got pregnant.

In my desperation, I confided in a trusted adult. When her daughter took me to the Health Department for a checkup, they told me I was six months pregnant. The trusted adult told me if I wanted to go to college, we would hide my pregnancy until the season ended.

I blocked those results out of my mind. I was the starting Point Guard and needed to lead my team to the South State, State, and Overall State Championships in Jackson, Mississippi. We won all three titles during my senior year. Because of my determination, I was selected to numerous All-Tournament teams throughout the state and Gulf Coast. They had no choice but to give me the Best Playmaker Award that year. I never shed any tears of joy or sadness; my accomplishments spoke past my weaknesses.

After my senior year, dozens of college coaches called to see where I committed to play. Dot told the coaches, "Bell has a baby and isn't going to play basketball at nobody's college." I always felt my mother's rage and disappointment over my pregnancy. I constantly begged that God would not allow this to be my new life. I started talking to Him as if He was in the room. I needed to leave Gulfport, but I didn't have money, a car, or help with my baby. I also didn't have anywhere to go. I prayed harder for a miracle for me to use my story to help others like me.

One day, I checked the mail, and there was a letter for me from the Mississippi Gulf Coast Junior College (MGCJC). Dot didn't allow us to open mail, so I hid the letter and read it later. It was admission paperwork to attend MGCJC on the Perkinston "Perk" campus in Wiggins, Mississippi. I thanked God for my miracle. I quickly completed and mailed the admission papers. Two weeks later, I received an acceptance letter from the college. Dot told me I wasn't going. She said my baby Katilya was my responsibility alone. Luckily, my grandfather was there when she read the letter. He told Dot, "Let her go and be your first child to attend college."

Dot agreed to let me attend and keep my daughter under certain conditions: I couldn't play sports, I returned home every weekend, I maintained a "C" average, and she'd receive all child support checks and extra money from the school. I easily agreed to her terms. I was fueled by my aunt's husband's hateful words, and I was on a mission to succeed.

On campus, I studied first and then walked over to the gym. I watched the guys play my game, but graduation was my priority. Two weeks passed, and I returned wearing my basketball shoes. Needless to say, I dominated the basketball court, and by the end of the night, they asked me to return the next day. I played daily after study sessions. My friends, Delisa and Arthurine, were always there cheering me on.

Rumors spread about the female point guard going toe-to-toe with the men. It drew in the guys who became comfortable with losing, members of the women's basketball team, and eventually, their coaches. Sports Hall of Fame Coaches Sue Ross and Blackie Smith invited me to watch the Lady Bulldogs' basketball practice. I remembered my agreement with Dot, but my roommate Renee advised me to just watch them practice, so I did. Afterward, Coach Ross asked for my opinion on the team. I told her they needed a leader. I soon realized I was that leader and that I could enhance the program.

Coach Ross changed my life; she answered my prayers and gave me hope again. She offered me a full two-year scholarship to play basketball. She gave me until Friday to give her an answer. When I thought of what Dot would do to me, the fear set in, but that didn't stop me.

That Wednesday, Arthurine and I drove from Perk to my oldest sister's house in Gulfport to gauge Dot's mood. I walked through the unlocked door to find my infant crying in my sister's house alone. Katilya was wet, hungry, and wearing the same clothes from that Sunday. I immediately brought her back to campus. I never called to let Dot know that I had my daughter, and she never called to say that Katilya was missing. They never apologized for abandoning my infant, and I never shed any tears because now I had to be a thinker for my baby.

God worked through my coaches to fix my situation. They placed me in the marriage housing on campus and provided baby food and supplies. My teammates even babysat when I went to class. Shout out to my 1978-80 Lady Bulldogs at Perk, Anita Madden, Mary Matunda, Betty McCune, and a host of other Perk friends who helped me at my lowest. In those two years, I grew spiritually and as a person, mother, and basketball leader. I received several awards there and played on the Junior College All-Star Team. Once, my aunt's husband told me that I was "going to end up barefoot, pregnant, and never going to amount to nothing." He always made sure I knew I was a nobody. He didn't say much when I graduated with an Associate degree with a 3.0.

After graduation, I lived with Dot. Her disposition was the same, but my mindset was different. I received a phone call from John May, a Gulfport native and Men's basketball player for the University of South Alabama. He said the university needed a Point Guard with my skills and took me to Mobile, Alabama, to visit South's campus. Coach Butler offered me a full two-year scholarship to play basketball for the Lady Jaguars, and I accepted immediately. I built trust that Dot could keep my daughter more safely this time.

Basketball at the University of South Alabama was different from my experience at Perk. I was the only African American on the team and our season wasn't exceptional. My senior season showed more promising results, but soon basketball was the least of my worries. Dot couldn't keep my daughter anymore. I had my daughter, basketball practice, and classes. I was a broke college student living in the dorms with my daughter until a better opportunity came. My friends Kelia, Denise, and J. Anthony helped as much as a student could. Not everyone was so helpful. My new roommate, another black woman, reported me for housing a child in the dorms. Following my eviction, I moved back home to Gulfport.

While back at home, I met my future husband, an AirForceman, at Keesler Air Force Base. After our union, my family received a military assignment to Turkey. When we toured the facilities, we, of course, found the Air Force Women's Basketball Team practicing. The Coach invited me to try out for the team. For five years, I played throughout Europe as their starting Point Guard.

Unfortunately, tragedy struck in Germany. While playing on the last night of a tournament, I tore my right ACL. After emergency surgery and recovery in a German hospital, my husband and I flew to Turkey and then home. After six months of rehabilitation, I trained hard for six more months. My sights were now set for the WNBA.

My high school basketball coach, Van Chancellor, was now the Coach for the Houston Comets' WNBA team. I received an invitation to try out, but even with my injury, the women were younger, faster, and had higher endurance. I hung up my basketball shoes and put on a Head Coaching hat.

After ending my 10-year marriage, I relocated to Atlanta, GA. I had a baby boy named Paris while there. My aunts encouraged me to finish my degree. My Aunt Rosan helped me realize that Dot didn't know how to show pride when I completed my degree.

My son Paris and I relocated to Mobile, AL, and after a 15-year gap, I re-enrolled at the University of South Alabama and earned a bachelor's degree in Education. I followed with a master's degree from the University of Mobile. I proudly educated the leaders of tomorrow, and they named me the Walmart Teacher of the Year. In recognition of my sports achievements, I received the Women in Sports Award and was inducted into the University of South Alabama Wall of Fame and the MGCJC Athletic and Gulfport Sports Halls of Fame. I am currently the only woman on the Gulfport Sports Hall of Fame Board.

My success came with conflict and setbacks. Still, remember, don't let someone determine your future. Have faith that you can follow your dreams; you will run into obstacles, but keep moving forward toward your destiny.

About Beverly Coleman

Beverly Coleman is a firm believer in community service and public education and has always strived for academic and sports excellence. While procuring an Associate's, Bachelor's and a Master's degree in teaching Physical Education for Pre-K through the 12th grade, she managed to raise two children and build a promising coaching career in Women's Basketball, Volleyball, Soccer, and Track & Field. She is a 3-time Hall of Famer and will proudly recount tales from her time as a Point Guard, but she began from humble beginnings.

She helped her mother to raise 3 of her 7 siblings in Gulfport, MS. There in North Gulfport, she discovered her love for basketball. It became her confidant and solace through teen pregnancy, single-parenthood, college athletics, and even a 5-year international semi-professional career. Unfortunately, due to a tragic injury, while playing basketball abroad, she was unable to sustain her trajectory toward playing for the WNBA. Instead of allowing her injury to end her love for basketball, she traded in her tennis shoes for a Coaching hat with the Mobile County Public School system. Now, she is a certified Adaptive Recreation & Sports Specialist and Special Needs Teacher. She spends her free time volunteering with the Special Olympics as a coach and a basketball referee in Mobile, AL.

DELILA HOUSE

Striving for Perfection, While Never Being Good Enough
By: Delila House

I can remember sitting in my third-grade teacher's class as she asked a question. Raise your hand if you think you are perfect. I slowly raised my hand, noticing that I was the only one in the room with my hand raised. I remember all the other kids laughing while I did not understand. I had a great relationship with my teacher, so after class, she explained that no one was ever perfect. I think that it sunk in, but not really. Thus began my life of always striving to be the perfect person, whether that was the perfect daughter, friend, or girlfriend. Little did I know that this would lead me down a path that left me broken, confused, and never feeling good enough for anything or anyone.

I constantly strived for the perfect grades. I was so hard on myself that my parents did not have to say anything. I went through grade school and high school, struggling with perfection. Never really understanding that it would never exist. I was not into the church as much in my younger age, so I was not aware of the relationship I was missing with God. I only had memories of the few times we were in church and the conversations I had with my grandmother. It was not that I thought my little town was bad, but more so that we had so much more potential than what it was. So, I thought that if I worked hard enough, I would be able to be the person that could change the life of my family. The relationship with my mother was helpful because she believed in me, and I could always count on her to keep me motivated. Because of this, I worked hard for everything important, constantly striving to do everything right.

Junior High and High school led to relationships that were hurtful and disappointing. This fed into my thought process of being the perfect girlfriend. I wanted to make sure their families liked me just as much as they did. If things begin to go wrong, I tried to figure out what it was about me that was wrong. I remember facing one break up and thinking as a teenage girl that life was over. In those teenage years, you face so many things, and you question everything that you know. I found myself thinking that there was nothing else to live for. In the middle of the night, when I knew my parents were asleep, I decided to end my life. A friend of mine, who I was talking to, notified my mom of what happened, and she quickly rushed me to the hospital. Of course, I had to stay overnight and set up a treatment plan to help monitor the things I had going on. I realized that I disappointed my mom. You could tell by the look on her face that she could not understand why or what was happening. Honestly, I did not either. The next morning, I was released from the hospital as if nothing had happened because the perfect lifestyle that I was formulating in my mind needed to be front and center again. Once I allowed this spirit in my life, it would take everything that I had to fight it off.

After graduating from high school, I continued striving for straight As and the best of the best while in college. I compared myself to others even though most people never knew that. Many people thought I was living this perfect life, so I guess my plan of striving for perfection was working in some weird way. Most people did not know that I constantly battled depression and suicidal thoughts because the door had been open to it during my high school years. I can remember being bullied and picked on just because I wanted so much out of life. I never understood why people judged you for wanting more. I was slowly hurting myself more and more emotionally. The relationship strain that I had with certain members of my family was only growing farther apart. I was emotional, and I held everything in because letting things out meant you were not perfect. Wow, thinking about that now makes me want to shed tears for that little girl I was inside, trying to understand life. I went through college developing more and more trust issues. I made some bad decisions, and that became a daunting factor for my future decisions. I was quiet but firm at the same time because I knew that I had to make a way out of no way. Work became my stress reliever. If there was not anything else that I was good at, it was work. I finished college, and then came my college graduation.

On the day of my college graduation, I was excited and thrilled that I had completed such a great accomplishment. My family came up, of course, to support me. My father had gotten sick during my college years. There were certain times that he would have these little episodes that were sometimes uncontrollable. That day I wanted to make sure he ate and got enough water because we would be outside for hours in May in the center of Mississippi. He told me that he was okay and not to worry. My name was called, and I walked across the stage to receive my bachelor's degree. This degree was not for me but for my family. After the ceremony was over and the graduates were meeting their families, I could not find mine. The stadium was big, but it could not be that big. I called my mom to see if I was overlooking them, and she informed me that they had to go back to my apartment. My heart dropped. I wanted to make them so proud. That day became a blur because there were no pictures to be taken or memories that you would want to last. I was devasted. When I think about it today, I realize that something drastic could have happened to my father, but it did not sink in that day. I just kept asking my mom why she would not stay there to see me when I walked off the field. She could have ridden back with me was the only thing that I was thinking because honestly, this degree was for her, not me. So, of course, you know what I did next. I went to work because work was the only thing I knew for sure I was good at.

Soon after my college graduation, I met a guy that would become my husband. I knew at the time of marrying him that the decision was not the best one, but if I called the wedding off, I would have to admit that I was not good enough and that I was not living this perfect little life. The next couple of years would be difficult for me because I became distant from those closest to me. I was slowly losing myself because I was trying to make my marriage work. I remember quitting a job that made more than I ever thought I would be coming straight out of college to go to a job that was paying minimum wage. This was a humbling experience because I had no idea what minimum wage was at the time. I was doing this for my husband, and so I thought it was best. I ended up pregnant during this time and having a miscarriage. If I had never experienced depression before, I was now. I remember feeling like I was killing my child myself and then looking in the mirror, asking why I was not good enough to be a mom. I had to face the reality that the child I had quickly grown close to was gone. I had several friends around me having babies, and it took everything I had to be happy for them. This sent me into the darkest moments of my life.

After the miscarriage, I got a divorce, and I was forced to figure life out again. I went years just working and pushing through because I could fix work, but I could not fix myself. I would go to therapists and feel like I was just sitting there talking while they were looking at the wall. Inside I was screaming, help me, you are the doctor. The next three years would spiral out of control. I started going to church less, I started distancing myself from family even more, and I started hanging in places that were not safe for me. I think about the times that I probably could have faced death if that little voice did not say do not go there. During this time, things happened that will affect me for the rest of my life. I did not know who I was anymore. And then one day, I woke up trying to figure out what happened and how I got there. The company I was working for gave me an opportunity to escape reality and focus on me. Then one day, it paid off. I knew that I needed to escape and get away from the city where I lived, so I did.

I sold the majority of everything that I had in my house and packed up the important things. I had to say goodbye to whoever and whatever I was at the time. I moved to Memphis, TN, to start a new journey and to have a new freedom. You hear many people say that you can move to a new city, but you will still have the same problems. I can say this, I had to battle through some of the same problems, but it was easier doing it with the right influence around me. My new job was exciting, and I was traveling so much. I ended up in another relationship that I felt was perfect at the time. In the summer of 2018, my dad had a heart attack, and my world stopped. I am a dreamer, and I feel things in the spirit, so I thought the pain I was feeling at the time had to do with what was going on with him. Little did I know that I was about to experience a health battle myself. Throughout my life, I battled with health issues. I had times were things would get bad, and then my doctors were able to fix them. This time was different. There were nights where I did not think I would wake up the next morning because I had so many different pains. It went from my heart to my lungs, to my legs, to my digestive system, to my thought process. I was no longer able to walk upstairs without being out of breath. I would crawl to bed at night because

I could not walk. I hid this a lot because I did not want anyone to feel sorry for me. After seeing several doctors, I was diagnosed with Fibromyalgia (a disorder characterized by widespread musculoskeletal pain accompanied by fatigue, sleep, memory, and mood issues). I remember crying in the doctor's office and at home because the doctor basically said I would have some good days and some bad. I went into 2019 thinking I would have the best year of my life, but before January ended, everything changed. I was faced with an illness that I had to learn to live with. I faced a breakup that I was not expecting, and my job was now taking a toll on me. At that time, I realized that there was no such thing as perfection. I was forced to face reality and learn how to fix myself. I cut off everyone and only focused on me. I did not want to talk to or see anyone. I worked all day and went home at night to cry myself to sleep. The thing that comforted me was no longer there. I could not work my way out of this.

I finally realized that the only thing that would prepare me for the rest of my life was my relationship with God. I started going to a counselor that truly challenged me to do things differently. She broke me down, but it was necessary for me to build myself back up. I needed to know what was causing so much of the past issues. Then I soon met some great friends to help me understand scripture and living for God completely. I needed people who could pray for me at that moment; I could not be the strong person that everyone was used to. I started writing my devotional and trying to figure out my true purpose in life. Those next six months, I became a different person. I started learning and researching how to live with Fibromyalgia. I developed my devotional time and my relationship with God. I let go of religion and what it was supposed to look like because that had me striving for perfection all along. I realized that my purpose was to help people and help them see who they really were. I published my *14 Day Devotional Friend I Got You* during the pandemic to help other people. For six months, I held on to it, not knowing why, but it came out right when people were looking for God. After publishing my book, I realized that being a leader and helping people through life is best. I worked to get my certification for Life and Leadership Coaching. I am now walking in my truth because I went through everything that I did. I am a speaker and coach with scars, and at times, my brain fog gets the best of me. The one thing that I do know is that I am here living out my God ordained purpose. I am graced for this and will continue to pull the best out of every assignment that God sends my way. I am a trainer, a leader, and a coach, and I am here to let people know that you do not have to strive for perfection. The longer you strive for perfection, you will never be good enough. Reach out to me for coaching services and go to my website www.delilashantea.com to purchase my devotional to start working on you today.

About Delila House

Delila is the owner of *Delila Shantea* and has worked in the multifamily industry over a decade. She specializes in training and development within her industry. She is a member of several organizations where she holds leadership positions. Her experience in public accounting and multifamily has allowed her to develop leadership qualities that she strives to share with the world. She decided to step out on faith and start her own business venture where she builds people and shows them how to be a leader, mentor, and friend. Her goal is to motivate people to be the best version of themselves, which led her to develop "Friend I Got You" in 2019. Her love for people and leadership also led her to pursue her coaching certification to become a Life and Leadership Coach. As a coach she is helping individuals and businesses enhance their leadership skills and find balance.

KIM SHELTON

Rebounding After Almost Certain Defeat
By: Kim Shelton

I am inspired by the legacy of my late parents, Willie Lee, Sr, and Thelma Nixon Shelton, to write this chapter. I am the sixth child of 10 born to the union of my parents. I was born on February 10, 1957, at my family's residence on Watts Street in a housing projects, Tulane Court.

It was one of many projects which were all Black as I grew up during the Segregation and George Wallace era. The projects at that time was the only housing Blacks could live in as few had enough money to buy homes. We grew up in communities full of decent families and quiet living. Even though the outside world looks down on them as ghettos of crime driven dens of poverty, my projects was not such a place.

Our household consisted of Daddy, Mama and five brothers and five sisters. We grew up in a family filled with love and good food. I remember living in the projects playing in the park, jacks, swinging on monkey bars and playing hide and seek. We could only go to the park after completing our household chores, making our beds and taking care of our personal hygiene.

Our parents instilled in us these Principles: Honor God always, treat people the way you expect them to treat you and always keep your word for it is your bond. I strive to embody these principles as I strive to encourage others to seek their full potential.

The neighborhood we moved to in 1970 was called Ridgecrest. There were whites' families that live on Ardmore Drive when we first moved there. I attended Bellingrath Junior High School, where I joined the band and learned how to play the clarinet. I also ran track, played basketball, volleyball and softball.

For most of my life, I had to wear the clothes my mother brought me from work. The Martin family owned a realtor state business; therefore, I dressed differently from other kids in the neighborhood. I wore expensive clothes until I could afford to buy my clothes. I wore shoes that had holes in them and normally used cardboard in them.

My mother was an excellent cook, and eating at our house was a feast each day. My mother, Thelma, came from a family of fourteen—12 children and Grandma Pearl and Grandpa Sam Nixon. I woke up to the smell of the aromas of coffee percolating in the coffee pot on the stove and delicious biscuits made from scratch in the oven. Fatback or skins, as we called it, along with scrambled eggs, cheese and grits was our standard meals.

I do remember one incident in my childhood that traumatized me. My brother had the usual friends, some of whom he had occasional fights with. One Christmas Day, he was on a curve where skaters showed off their new skates and skated up and down the blocked street. He was skating and got into a fight, and this boy and his older brother doubled teamed him. My brother ran home and got a knife to protect himself. He got into another fight with the brothers, and the younger brother was stabbed and died on the way to the hospital

Our family had to move because of this incident. My brother was sent to a Reformatory school at the age of eight. He had just turned eight on December 8. He was released at the age of 13, and prior to his coming home, and so did the dead boy's family.

We moved from Tulane Court to Trenholm Court, which meant new schools and making new friends. I was devasted by the whole incident, as well as my family. I wonder if the time away from his family hurt him at such a young age. I chose not to talk about it and suppressed my shame. As I write this chapter, tears are streaming down my face as the pain still breaks my heart. It took me almost 30 years to talk about what happened that day and the negative impact it had on my selection of men to be involved with. Every man I dated, other than my daughter's father, had been to jail. I dived into my school work and excelled in my classes, making the Dean's List and joined ROTC.

We moved from Trenholm Court to the section known as Ridgecrest, which still had white families living on Ardmore Dr. That area is now all Black and today is still our family home.

I wanted to work to be able to buy my own clothes. I had a relative, Aunt Elizabeth, one of my Mom's older sisters, who owned an eating business. The Colonial Grill. I wanted to work so that I would not wear hand-me-down clothes and have money to buy things a young teenager need. I spent every weekend, evening, and summer from age 12 to 16 working for Aunt Elizabeth and Uncle Jabo.

I meet many people while working there, one of whom I took a liking to. This man was fifteen years older than me. I sneaked around and fell in love with this guy, Eugene Jeter. I got pregnant and gave birth to my only child. My daughter, whom I named Kimberly, was 9 pounds and 5 ounces. Her father paid my hospital bill, and I could attend school because of my scholastic skills.

In my Senior Year, I got a job with the summer program because I took typing and shorthand. I knew these skills would help me get a job, and I was blessed and hired that summer as a Summer Aide at Maxwell Air Force Base in Montgomery, Alabama.

My base supervisor was impressed with my job performance and work ethics that I was given a Stay in School Position. I would work 20 hours a week when school was in and 40 hours a week when school was out. While working this job on the Base, it gave me the drive to join the military and one day serve my country.

Growing up in the Shelton's household, you were given two options after graduation from high school. You could join the military or go to college. I applied to my hometown HBCU, The Alabama State University, and was accepted. I hit the campus, all ready to party and get a degree. As a Freshmen, one of my girlfriends, Rosa Turner, invited me to a party at Ramada Inn. It was at the Ramada that I met Glenn, one handsome sharp dressed man. I was in love. Although my girlfriend Brenda grew him from Hunter Station begged me not to date alone marry Glenn, I persisted.

My life changed as I found out I might have been smart in my books, but I had zero street sense as my father and mother sheltered us from that environment.

My years in college were rough because of all the abuse I was going through. I was blessed to receive a four-year ROTC Scholarship with full tuition, and books were provided free of costs. All of that would fade as my grades dropped, and I made my first D in Economics class. Too afraid I stayed in the marriage while in college. Ever heard the expression "God takes care of babies and fools"? He went back to jail, and I used that time to raise my grades and was back on course for graduation.

On August 25, 1979, I graduated from Alabama State University with a Bachelor of Science Degree in Computer Information Systems. I was assigned to report to Active Duty at Keesler AFB, Oct 1979. I would be enrolled in a 36 weeks computer programming course with a follow-on assignment to Offutt AFB, Nebraska. My oldest brother Jack drove me to Keesler AFB to report for active duty.

My husband visited me at the Base and was issued a military ID Card. I pleaded with him not to steal anything, especially on the military base. Imagine my shock sometime later when I was handed a note asking me to report to Security Police. I was written up and phased out of my computer course. I was embarrassed and had to seek counseling. Because of the amount of money the Air Force had spent on me, I was given a second chance and able to stay in the Air Force. I was enrolled in the Administration Management course.

I was assigned to the 3391, 3394 and the Avionics Maintenance Squadron the four years I was at Keesler. There were few black officers assigned to Keesler. I was called the N-word a few times, but it did not deter me from completing my training. This girl from the projects was being saluted any time she walked on the base by enlisted personnel, even if they were white. All I wanted to do was to do my four years and get out of Mississippi. As an Officer, I was not allowed to associate with my enlisted personnel, only officers. I had to adjust to the rules of the Air Force.

My supervisor Captain Bailey had a problem with me playing basketball with the enlisted women. Even though there were male officers and no regulation that said I could not play, he said I would never make Captain. I got a notice stating that I did not make the Captain list. My separation date from active duty would be February 28, 1984.

After separation from the Air Force, I sought employment and took whatever job I could as I was a single parent, and my child and I had to survive. I worked as a Substitute Teacher by name request at the Alternate School. I also worked as a Desk Clerk at Muse Manor until I was selected for a full-time NAF job at the Bowling Alley until 1998.

Life takes unexpected curves, and my mother, Thelma, got sick, so I resigned to go home to help care for her. She died on August 28, 1989. Talk about unwanted tests; I was shaken to my very core. No longer would I hear her comforting voice, her explanation of things and that never-ending love.

I was told to report to my new job in March, two months before my daughter, Kimberly's high school graduation. My friend Rachel Mack introduced me to the world of federal Contacting, and because of my education, she knew I would qualify for civil service jobs.

My journey began with the Department of Army Corp of Engineers in New York City, and Rachel allowed my daughter to live with her when I reported to work. I started as a GS-5 and was promoted to the ranks of GS-7, GS-9, and GS-11 Contract Specialist Intern. New York presented its unique set of job integrity. Most of the employees did not have college degrees, and I encountered all types of hardship because of my promotions.

I cried many days and nights as I missed my only child and family in Alabama. I never knew there were such mean and jealous people in the world until I moved to New York. I did have enough faith to know that God did not bring me this far to give up on me or leave and go back home. I stayed and started dating a younger guy.

In love again, I married for the second time in 1994. Theo was trained in computer service and had taught himself well enough to make a living. Together, we started our own woman-owned small business: The S&L (Shelton/Lewis) Computer Service. We ventured out on Wall Street, and we sold computers, and he set up networks for businesses. Everything was fine until our fifth year of marriage, when he started staying out and having affairs. It was verified one Sunday. I went to church, and he remained home as he had arrived just minutes before I was to leave for church. The business phone rang and when I answered a female asked: "who was I"? I replied that I was his wife, and she hung up the phone. When I confronted Theo, he assaulted me and fractured my jaw. I called the Police and had him arrested. I divorced him the same year.

After ten years and no promotion with the Corp of Engineers in July 2001, I was selected GS-12 Team Leader with the Department of Army, Brooklyn, New York. For some reason, I started praying to God more, which continued for one year before the promotion. Among my prayers to God was for a transfer out of 26 Federal Plaza. I live in New Jersey, and the train ride was grueling, and I had to pass through The World Trade Center to get to work

On September 11, 2001, I went through the World Trade Center one hour before the first plane hit the First Tower. God gave me grace and favor that day because he had work for me to do. I was able to train my staff and help them secure their FAC-C Certifications and warrants. I was selected for NH-3, Pay band position in Virginia. I worked for nine months and was given an opportunity to relocate close to home.

I received a Contracting Specialist position at Fort McPherson, East Point, Georgia. With the base line closure deadline, I rejoined the Veterans Administration in August 2006 and moved to Pensacola, Florida. Six months later, I was reassigned to the Biloxi/Gulfport VA Medical Center.

I spent 17 years preparing for the Supervisory Contracting Officer position that I was selected for in Montgomery, Alabama, and only by the grace of God, I got it. I know that all things are possible for those who believe, and without God, I never would have made my way back to Montgomery, Alabama, as a GS-13 Branch Chief.

Born and raised in the Tulane and Trenholm Courts projects in Montgomery, Alabama, to now living a life of purpose and faith is all the results of strong faith and a loving family of ten. I firmly believe that it matters not where you come from but How you Walk your own path to success. Your walk must be exemplified with virtue and integrity.

I will use my work experiences and personal social contacts to help the youth of my community to the Best that God allows me to do. My nonprofit organization will mentor young boys and girls in overcoming social obstacles, educational deficiencies and attaining a scholarship to have a better life.

In closing, walk your walk and shine brightly, for no man can take what God gave you.

For inquires or personal appearances, please contact me at mskimshelton@walkurwalk.com. or domain name walkurwalk.com

About Kim Shelton

Kim Shelton is a Leader, Mentor and Veteran from Montgomery, Alabama. She strives to push others to see their full potential. She has one Daughter (Kimberly), two Grandchildren (Kianna and Timothy) and a great Grandaughter (Kori). She earned a Master's Degree in Information Management System from Central Michigan University and a Bachelor of Science in Computer Information System from Alabama State University. At graduation, she earned her commission and was appointed as a 2nd Lt in the USAF assigned to Keesler AFB. She began working in the Acquisition Field in 1993. Her journey began as an Intern with the Army Corp of Engineers, New York. She accepted the challenge of a new career and culture. She completed her internships also worked in Virginia, Fort McPherson, Pensacola and the Biloxi VA. She spent 17 years preparing for the Supervisory Contracting Officer position and only by the grace of God, she got it. She retired November 2018 with 40 years of Federal Service.

FALLEN CHERICE PIZARRO

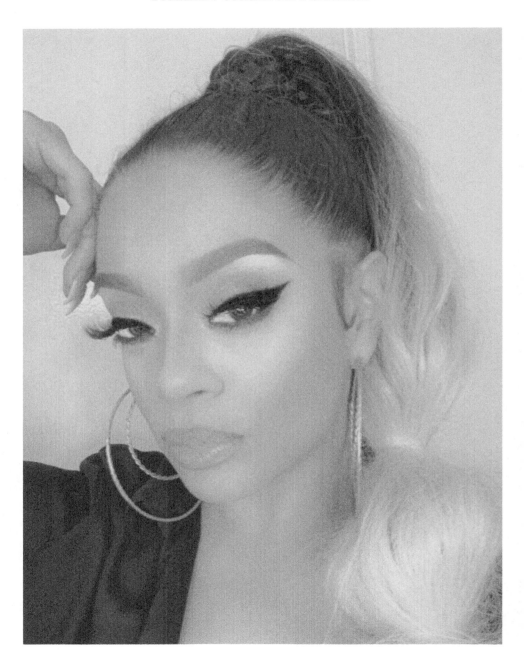

Dreamer of Dreams

By: Fallen Cherice Pizarro

WHO I AM

I am Fallon Pizarro, a 38-year-old 80's baby from Chicago, the most beautiful city in the world. I have lived all over Chicago. I grew up in most of the north side called the jungle. Trust me, it was the jungle for real. I was the only child for 14 years. Multi-biracial, multi-faceted. With a background of Black, Puerto Rican, Indian, and Irish, I always knew I was a little different growing up. I looked different than everyone else. Hence, I always got bullied.

I started dancing very young. As a child, I remember walking by Miss Lyn's Dance Academy right off Morse Street. I told my mom, *"mom, I really want to dance; I want to take these classes"*. So, she signed me up. This was a big deal coming from my culture, because all the other girls honestly were not really into anything. I realized growing up in Chicago as a kid we really did not have sports or things that we could indulge in to to keep us out of trouble. So, dancing was an outlet for me to keep on a straight path.

MALE ROLE MODELS, NOT REALLY

Growing up as an only child with my mother, it was not always the easiest, some of my hardest, if not the hardest relationship. I had witnessed my father of abusing her at a young age. I remember, being five years old and asking him to not come back around because every time he had come, he would be angry and punch holes in the wall. I decided, I do not need him in my life. I pushed him away.

I remember he came to school one day when I was in fourth grade, but he was not on the parents sign up list. The Chicago Public Schools thought it was okay, so they took me out of class because they thought I was going to be happy to see him. I was furious that they even let him in the building. That was the last time I saw him. I heard from him in eighth grade. He promised to take me Christmas shopping, that didn't happen and never heard from him again.

My mother was in relationship with my little brother's father, which was very toxic. He was a drug dealer, and he was very abusive to her. Some of the incidents I remember such as the first time he hit her; he slapped her in the living room of our Section 8 apartment. There were so many roaches that I literally broke out in hives from them. I was constantly in fear. I would always defend her from him. I remember one time I wanted to go out with my friends. They were fighting again. I came rushing and hit in the side of his face with a 2x4. Before that incident, I tried to burn him with iron. I held a knife to him like this was not the first incident, this was just the worst. During that time, I just wished she would leave this man. What is he doing for us?

THE LIGHTS OF MY LIFE

My grandfather was the best "positive" role model in my life. But he was also a big drug dealer. And I respected him because he loved me so much. I was fascinated with the life because I honestly that was all I knew, I was his Grand Queenie. He barely knew English, did not know how to read, or write and had a big Puerto Rican accent.

My Grandma was my true rock! She taught me everything, she was very smart and read a lot which made me become a strategic reader. I owe a lot of my personality to her, my elegance, wittiness and sarcasm. I would stay with her from time to time when things weren't the easiest at my home.

My little brother was born when I was 14, freshman in high school and that was my first child. I took that little boy everywhere, even had a carrier. When he was first born, my mom had a cesarean, so I had to do all the night feedings. I never even changed a diaper before. I had to sleep on the sofa with his bassinet next to me and this little boy could only sleep on his stomach, which I was always so terrified about so I could barely get any sleep. I was so tired going to school the next day, but I would have to lay him on top of me for him to go to sleep. I think that is where my natural mothering quality came from.

BACK TO DANCE

I continued dancing all the way through College. In high school my mom heard on the radio; they are doing a casting for Save the Last Dance which was being filmed in Chicago. So, I was hired on as a background. And then they asked me to be Bianca Lawson's second team, which basically I would do all kinds of lighting and anything for her, but I got paid extra for it, and it was cool. I felt like I was a celebrity. Like whom else was cutting Paramount checks at 17 years old. After that, I attended Columbia College Chicago. I took a split major, interdisciplinary studies in Dance and Entertainment management. I thought I was going to be a star. But to be honest, I always had the star dreams without the grittiness of becoming the JLo or the Beyonce because the drive within was not enough. I did not have the push that I wish I had coming from my family.

At 20, a college classmate told me about an R. Kelly video casting they held down at his Chocolate Factory. I was very nervous because auditioning was not really a thing that I liked. In spite of my fears, I made it, I got the video, and it was an intense two months of 9pm to 6am rehearsals. This video was supposed to be epic. However, it was coming out during his sex scandal. The video comes out and I was working at the Sears Tower in the souvenir photos area. I remember my managers were so excited for me being in the video they called me into the office to watch it. I thought I caught my big break but unfortunately let distractions take over.

BALLIN'

My life is always surrounded by movies as my inspiration because that is where my mind goes, to the fantasy land of the theater. I started bartending at this big club called Estate after falling in love with the movie Coyote Ugly. I was the only and token black girl. I remember I was bartending in VIP for every NBA, NFL, Pro League or whoever, and was very clueless to the fact. I had a couple, big named, customers. I mean, I literally had Michael Jordan's number on speed dial. All I have to do is shake up some Belvedere, strain it, and I am getting an obscene amount of money tonight; mostly because he wanted to take me home but I wasn't all about my money.

So that was the same time I met my husband, now wasband, Eddie Robinson. He played for the Chicago Bulls at the time, but I had no idea. I remember we were making googly eyes at each other the whole night and me being so green just turned 21 I had no idea that real celebrities would hang with us, you know, common folk. He finally approached me. We hit it off. We started having a blast, I was at every game and would travel to other cities to watch him play. It was good, genuine fun. Somewhere along the line it gets a little more serious and it is not so much fun anymore.

THE VISION

We moved to Houston, now I'm raising his son and was pregnant with my own son. After I gave birth, started dancing again and heard Beyonce was doing a casting for an all-girl band. I remember taking all these intense, heel classes to prepare but I could not maintain it. While I was pregnant with my son, I cracked my pelvic bone. I could not continue, as it was so painful that I just could not do the moves like I used to. I was sad because I felt like my dance career was over. But one thing that carried me through was my love for performing and the arts. Through dance, we always had to wear makeup and costumes so that is where my love for makeup fashion started.

Me and my husband were kind of living the life. We were going to the Grammys and the BET awards, red carpets and everything. We traveled to Vegas, LA, New York and wherever. I remember, I would get my makeup done for an event but would always come home and tweak it to something different. My husband would ask me "why don't you just do makeup?". 15 years ago, no one was doing makeup like that, then bam, it is now a YouTube and Instagram phenomenon. There was not even an Instagram when I started doing makeup

THE FALL

I finally had my little girl. I was complete – I had 2 boys and a girl. I opened a children's clothing boutique, Kiss my Couture Kids. I had an idea of creating this amazing space where it was visually pleasing for parents and kids. It had a cafe where the kids could go hang out in the back. An event space within the unit that had a runway. Kids could have birthday parties and all kinds of other gatherings like fashion shows. It was my blood sweat and tears. Unfortunately, we crashed and burned because one, we were a year behind because we had to sue our former contractors, so we were low on a lot of money, and two, I was wearing all the hats from maintenance man, to buyer, to cashier.

On top of this, I found out that we are broke and my husband was cheating. I did not have any more money to keep throwing at the business. I lost everything like my family's financial stability, my wishes, my dreams, my marriage, just everything. It was just gone. Like all together. Like in one click, vanished. I was so defeated. I did not allow the depression to hit me as it could. I tried to work hard on being and doing whatever I could do to save my marriage but it didn't work.

When we separated, we had $60,000 in our joint account and it was all the money we had left out of millions. I split the money and I was paying all the bills. He went from being an NBA player to never playing in the NBA again. He played in other leagues, but never made any money. Through it all, I would always push him to do more because I always wanted to push myself to do more.

The worst was finding out we were being evicted and had two days to move. I sold my wedding ring set to give us more time and pay for us to move. We took everything we can possibly get out of that house, the rest was put on the lawn by Sherif's orders. I cried. I do not like crying. My mom was sad, and my kids were confused. The whole time my husband was in Las Vegas because auditioning for the next season of the Big3. I did not get any money from him, nor did I get any help.

LIVE ANOTHER DAY

He proposed to his mistress while we were getting evicted. The day after we completed the move, he sent $1,700 for the down payment on the new place. We were there already; it had already been done. If I would have waited for him, we would have been out on the streets. His mother and sister lived in Houston while he relocated to Canada. I did not get any help from them. I never understood how you could go from taking the kids to school, making breakfast on the weekends to just never here and never around? These are our children. It is like I was not ever a wife. The treatment that I get between him, his family and my oldest son's Mother, you would think I was not raising her child for years and that I was the one that cheated.

When we first separated, I started working at Mac because I knew I was going to have to work at what I do best. I really strived at Mac. I started as a freelancer and quickly became permanent and a third key. I was booking photoshoots and other gigs. I started a business, IntoxiCandy, alcohol infused desserts. I felt like it was a new beginning for me. I could not really put myself out there while being in my marriage, without being accused of doing something that I was not doing probably because he was the one doing it. The reality of my life hit me. You are no longer basketball wife - cool. This man does not really want to be in our children's life like he should - not cool. We have got to move on.

I'm now focusing on my Creative Consultant business. I strive for, continuity, perfection, uniqueness, the exotic, the tantalizing. I want to have my hands into everything. I like to say I am the urban Martha Stewart. I could see me with my own kitchen utensils, my own everything. I can go into any business or event and figure out the outcome would have been better with my twist on it. We all have ideas especially when it comes to business and whether they be small or large. My job is to come in as the fixer, the one who fine-tunes every detail to perfection. You give me an inch and I'll run a marathon!

What is next? I was working at Mac four years and recently quit after the pandemic. I realized what my time is worth, what I am worth, and all my losses are only driving me into being the person that I need to be. It is never too late to revamp your life. I waited too long but now, I see it as marinating. It is trial and error. It is learning experiences. I have had a lot of those. I am still learning, and I love the fact that I can still grow. I can still say that I can keep evolving to the next level while creating levels you've never imagined in your dreams.

About Fallen Cherice Pizzaro

Fallen Cherice Pizzaro is a Beauty Consultant and Creative Genius.

She was born and raised in Chicago. During her early age, she has been a creative child who loves arts and drawings. Not only that, she started dancing jazz, tap, and ballet when she was 4 years old and quickly worked her way up to advance levels. She went on to become a lead dancer in her hair dance production.

She then enrolled to Columbia College Chicago majored in Dance and Entertainment Management to get her degree.

After college, Fallen moved to Houston to start a family with her 2 children.

She started Kiss My Bootyque,MUA. Her love for makeup started as a young girl with influence from her grandmother and Elaborate looks for Dance performances. Now that she has acquired all the knowledge and experiences, she is now running MUA for directing and styling photo and video shoots. Moreover, she planned elaborate birthday parties for her family, and soon enough, others discover how amazing her works and went to her to plan and direct their events.

Whatever the idea, she knows how to take it to another level. As her mantra goes *"Give me an inch and I'll run a marathon"*

Her journey went on and she opened KISS My Couture Kids. It is a children's clothing boutique and event space. She hosted children's, birthday parties, fashion shows, and other events in her boutique.

With all her successes in life, she has also rough times which measured how strong she has become. After her divorce, she found herself being a single mother in need of a 9-5. She dealt this situation as a strong individual and a willful mother. So she went with the field she knows best and applied for M.A.C

Through her time at M.A.C., she made many connections that helped catapult her many businesses. These are:

- Intoxicandy: alcohol infused cupcakes and treats),
- Prague: pop on ponytails)
- Kiss my Bootyque: MUA, styling, overall creative consultant.

Using social media as a creative outlet, Fallen let all aspects of her genius sore. Visual editor, fashion stylist, not forgetting her comedic personality and "I mean what I say" approach in life.

She is "The Urban Martha Stewart" as she always say, *"I want to be a household name, having products and solutions for every aspect of life, beauty, fashion, home, relationships, events and more".*

-Creative Child, arts, drawing

-Started dance at 4yrs old (jazz, tap, ballet)

-Quickly worked her way up to advance levels.

-Went on to become a lead dancer in her hair dance production

-Columbia College Chicago (majored in dance and entertainment management)

-After College Fallon moved to Houston to start a family. 2 children

-Her love for makeup started as a young girl with influence from her grandmother and Elaborate looks for Dance performances.

-Started Kiss my Bootyque, MUA

-MUA, Directing and styling photo and video shoots

-Planned elaborate birthday parties for her family, soon others went to her to plan their events.

-Whatever the idea, she knows how to take it to another level

-"Give me an inch and I'll run a marathon"

-Opened KISS my Couture Kids, Childrens clothing boutique and event space

-Hosted Childrens, bday parties, fashion shows and other events in her boutique

-After a rough divorce she found herself being a single mother in need of a 9-5, so she went with the field she knows best and applied for M.A.C

-Through her time at MAC she made many connections that helped catapult her many businesses

-Intoxicandy (alcohol infused cupcakes and treats)

-Prague "pop on ponytails"

-Kiss my Bootyque: MUA, styling, overall creative consultant.

-Using social media as an creative outlet, Fallon let all [OBJ] aspects of her genius [OBJ]sore

-Visual editor, fashion stylist, not forgetting her comedic personality and "I mean what I say" approach on life

-"The Urban Martha Stewart"

-"I want to be a household name, having products and solutions for every aspect of life, Beauty, fashion, home, relationships, events and more"

GLORIA WALTON

The Journey

By: Gloria Walton

Transformational Coach, Licensed Minister, Serial entrepreneur

Jeremiah 29:11 [11]**For I know the plans I have for you," declares the LORD, "plans to prosper you and not to harm you, plans to give you hope and a future."**

My name is Gloria Walton, and these are a few pages into my journey of self-discovery and a warning to women not to allow others' complacency to infringe upon their hopes and dreams. But against all odds, be your authentic self and live in the healthy space of possibilities. Believe in miracles and grow in wisdom and the wealth that God has destined you for.

At age twelve, my mother, escaping domestic violence, moved from South Carolina to New Jersey. We lived in the projects with my maternal aunts until our apartment in Montgomery Housing Projects. Living in the projects was a culture shock. I had never lived in an apartment or rode an elevator, jumped double dutch rope, or smelled marijuana before. I promised myself I would never let the projects define me. Filled with self-determination and passion, that against all odds, I would be successful, my own boss and wealthy. There was an energy and belief that nothing was impossible. Yes, I could do anything. I did not calculate the impact of others, minimizing my vision. Dream busters from afar are not as detrimental as the dream killers closest to you, speaking words of doubt and death into your life.

At age sixteen, I entered Montclair State University, my one-way ticket out of Montgomery Projects. Thankful to God and exploding with expectations, ready to conquer the world. By age twenty-two, I was a mother and happily married. We owned a single and multi-family dwelling. I knew real estate was one of our best options to build wealth. Although I had a college degree and a social service career, they limited my earning capacity. My plans for early retirement and traveling the world with my children seemed an impossibility. Although my husband had a well-paying job, I had a burning desire for over two houses, lovely jewelry, and new cars.

We had the perfect family; except I was dying inside. I could not accept a retired life on Social Security. What would be my daughter's inheritance? The housing market crashed, and although a disaster for many, I knew investing wisely and purchasing as many residential and commercial properties as possible could begin my desired portfolio. My husband decided he did not want to buy any more houses, especially in the NJ downtown area. That caused an internal struggle. I had to fight the many inner voices and the voice of my mother telling me I could do anything and never leave my future in the hands of anyone. I smothered a dream to appease someone else's limitations. I could have purchased independently, but I honored his wishes and took on a third job instead. A full-time social worker, on-call after hours, and weekend youth counselor.

Working for another will never give you the freedom, the abundance you desire, or that overflow the bible speaks of. I felt like I was swimming in the sea of mediocrity. Negative self-talk telling me to forget it, all those dreams are dead, and you have accomplished nothing. Unfortunately, there was an element of truth. You see, the thief had entered my home, using drugs, divorce, and death, to steal my hope. Drugs and alcohol were destroying the men in my life; divorce was the only option.

Now divorced I could make independent decisions, but the real estate window of opportunities was now closed. Raising my daughter and taking custodial responsibility for my niece and nephew left no room for a social life. I was emotionally spent and physically drained from working three jobs. The enemy tried my faith. I allowed the thought of suicide to enter my ear gate. That was a nonnegotiable short-lived thought. Realizing there was a crack in my faith, I ran to God. Remembering what my mother told me as a child, "Tell God Everything," I did just that. I poured my heart out to God. I cried to God about my disappointments, fatigue, hopes, and dreams that seemed dead.

Guilt plagued me about my financial condition. Yes, I had money, but it was not the inheritance I desired for my daughter, niece, or nephew. The more I talked to God the better I felt. My faith increased, and I had a new love relationship with God. My work routine and responsibilities did not change. But my hope was restored. God revived the vision he had given me and gave me favor with a local congregation. Where my knowledge of God and his principles for a successful life became my daily quest, my spiritual gifts were manifesting, and I could hear God!

I knew it was God because I did not think of myself to be qualified or spiritually mature enough to accomplish many of the tasks he put before me. Every challenge seemed impossible and required more of my time, talents, and resources. I received many compliments and achievement awards for feeding the hungry, visiting the jails, developing social justice, women, and youth ministries. The problem was, I did not see any of it as unique. I only did what was in my heart and followed God's instruction to completion.

Meanwhile, I still had my questions. God, when am I going to start the journey to fulfill my purpose, be my own boss, build wealth and good inheritance for my children? *"But thou shalt remember the LORD thy God: for it is he that giveth thee power to get wealth, that he may establish his covenant which he swore unto thy fathers, as it is this day,"* (Deuteronomy 8:18 KJV)

On June 1, 1988, my job allowed me to visit Rahway State Prison. That decision changed the trajectory of my life. Soon afterward, I began transporting youth to Rahway's' Scared Straight Program, working with families of prisoners, advocating for children's visitation rights, etc.; being a voice for the voiceless became a passion. There has been nothing more fulfilling than helping others find their path, reuniting families, and witnessing the transformation of others, physically, mentally, spiritually, and emotionally. The value of people is more significant than money and more satisfying than desserts. I understand that God's purpose for our lives is so much greater than we know. Conversing with my mother months before she died, she shared some childhood episodes. Where I would intervene in situations, she whispered, smiling, "you have always been a social worker, helping and being concerned about people. I know you think you a scientist but, no baby, you are a social worker at heart". My response was right, but social workers are broke ma.

Diagnosed with colon cancer in 1987 she survived the first surgery. In 1988 Bethesda Baptist Church sponsored a seven-day trip to Hawaii. She had never traveled out of the United States and she wanted to go. I paid for Cousin Ricky to escort her. They had a marvelous time. Unfortunately, it was the last plane ride she would take. At our August 1989 family reunion, she prophetically confessed that "some of us will not be here next year." The doctors were so sure they had removed all cancer, but instead, that dreadful disease returned and eventually spread to her brain.

She begged to come home, so I hired several shifts of private nurses and transported her to my house. The doctor explained that cancer was the worst pain anyone could experience. I dreaded going home to watch her suffer and slowly fade away. Johnathan was eight months and just learning to crawl. I'randa, my daughter, and niece Tawana were in grammar school. They would talk with her, sneak her peppermint candies, and make sure she had water by her bed. She loved all five of her grandchildren. I would lay by her at night, read the scriptures, and brush her hair. Some nights, I would be so tired after cooking dinner that all I could do was sit near and stare at her. It was somehow still comforting, knowing my mother was still alive. Her condition grew increasingly worse, and I had to make the most painful decision of my life. I could no longer keep my mother at home. She returned to JC Medical Center for the last time. On April 8, 1990, my birthday, I left the hospital, and within an hour after an overnight stay, the hospital called to notify me of her death. Determined to keep the last two promises I made to her, which was to bury her in South Carolina near her mother and raise Jonathan and Tawana until it was safe to return them to their mother.

Because of a job-related accident, I could no longer do field investigations. I was out of work for three years. I put my vision book away, sold most of the furniture, placed sentimental items in storage, and gave the rest away.

I'randa went to her dad's, Jonathan and Tawana to their mother, and I took a flight to Arizona to begin a new life. I surveyed the land, filled out housing applications, and returned to New Jersey. Within approximately three weeks, the landlord approved an application for a beautiful apartment. In 1992, I made a conscious decision to walk away from what I once thought to be my future. I walked away from all my NJ properties. I moved to Arizona with my children and began a new life. Unable to work, I attended University of Arizona and received a grant writing certificate. I had settled with writing grants for faith- based organizations and non-profits. The following year I received an opportunity to return to work as the Intake Screener which required no fieldwork. Initially, I did not take the job. Since I was cleared to work, I remained in Arizona and got a counseling job with Arizona's incarcerated youth gang population.

Arizona's heat did not improve my back, but it helped my daughter's asthma. Shortly after the children's school year ended, we returned to a two-family home in NJ. Ten years later, Denise and I returned to Family Court, and the Judge returned custodial custody of her two children. The words of the Judge did not resonate immediately. He said, "whatever you did to reunify this family, without getting DYFS involved, you should sell it."

That was the voice of God. God used the Judge's words "you should sell it" to redirect my focus back to owning my business. It was also apparent that valleys are purposeful, and that inner voice of defeat is a liar. The heartaches, divorce, losses, and pain were necessary parts of the journey toward becoming my authentic self so that I could walk in my purpose.

In Getting There, David Limerick says, *"destiny is a journey to be enjoyed and that the proverbial "There" is found in walking out the journey of your life. David teaches you how to change your mindsets and to receive peace that comes with knowing you are walking out your purpose and destiny."[1]*

The journey led me through a challenging self-awareness process where my misery became my ministry, and I have welcomed my servant-leader mantle. I am a homeowner twice; God gave me back double with the clarity of my earthly assignment. My daughter is a business owner and living her best life.

The journey has given me confidence to become a Serial Entrepreneur, a better parent, the ability to accept love, and create a pathway to building a greater inheritance for my daughter. I have been fortunate to coach hundreds of men and women through a successful personal, spiritual, and professional transformation process. As founder of the Most Excellent Way Learning Life Centers Inc., a Family Reunification Center. Providing housing, behavioral health services, financial literacy and family reunification services to males and females ex-offenders.

Candidates are those struggling with change, addictions, divorce, or family court issues. Entrepreneurial Success through Emotional Intelligence online trainings are available for the community at large

To reach others looking for solutions to break self-destructive habits through a spiritual recovery process, I hosted "Something of Substance." Which quickly became a favorite Sunday evening local TV show. To expand the audience, God led me to develop the Urban Behavioral Health Services Inc., an ambulatory addictions clinic. The journey expanded across the country and to international communities where my integrated coaching approach of merging the social sciences and the Word of GOD into a

---

[1] Getting There, David Limerick, Carpenter's Son publishing (September 8, 2014)

workable model to transform broken lives into vessels of glory for God's use.

Still, on the journey, and God birthed Mothers & Daughters–N- Touch Outreach. A family preservation program that seeks to prevent girls from out-of-home placements, youth employment, and mentorship to women and their daughters. The coaching module is an incredibly positive spiritual force in the life of hundreds of women.

Women who come to the program with a myriad of family problems that led them to substance abuse, child abuse, domestic violence, unemployment, homelessness, and incarcerations. Upon program completion, we have witnessed the manifestation of transformed lives.

Mothers and Daughters have expanded into the virtual world. My daughter I'randa and I host a weekly Thursday evening podcast, "Mother's & Daughter's Candid Conversations."

My written work is now available on amazon. Mothers & Daughters Candid Conversations with God, a Seven-day devotional and writing exercises identifying the God-given power and authority of the mother's voice. Scripturally based to encourage and challenge mothers and daughters to strengthen, reconcile, and value their relationships. It gives mothers empowering declarations to break the power of negative spiritual influences.

It has been a great experience to be an In Command co-author.

If you are suffering in silence, unsatisfied, stagnant, unproductive, afraid of change or interested in starting a nonprofit, but do not know where to start, Email me at gwalton@mostexcellentwaylifecenter.com for a free fifteen-minute discovery call. Or schedule a fifteen- minute discovery call at www.mostexcellentwaylifecenter.com

About Gloria Walton
Transformational Coach, Licensed Minister, Serial entrepreneur

CEO/founder of the Most Excellent Way Learning Life Centers, a nonprofit. Previously featured in Women's Day Magazine, and Inside Edition. To offer spiritual recovery to a greater audience, Rev. Walton hosted a Sunday evening TV program, "Something of Substance." Founder of the Urban Behavioral Health Services Inc., a for-profit ambulatory addictions clinic. Rev. Walton's ministry has taken her into international communities where she is regarded as an expert on merging the disciplines of the social sciences and the Word of GOD into a workable model to transform broken lives.

Founder of Mothers and Daughters Outreach, a family preservation program seeking to prevent girls out of home placements. Women's empowerment and mentorship. Her written aid can be found in the co-authored spiritual journal Love, Peace and Joy and Mothers and Daughters Candid Conversation with God. Podcast Host, Mothers & Daughters Candid Conversation. Upcoming release "Living Louder Than Your Pain"

KRISTEN FENRICK

UnMasking the Truth

By: Kristen Fenrick

I was born on October 31, 1971. This is definitely an ordinary occurrence as we all have a birthday—that special day that we enter this world. What's different for me is I don't have any cute birth stories. I don't have any stories about my childhood or baby pictures or anything that would indicate a life for me before age five. I was adopted as a child, and the family that I was adopted into has always been elusive when it comes to topics of my birth, adoption, and pretty much anything that has to do with the truth. I have no idea who I was or what my life was prior to the one picture I have of myself in a McDonald's parking lot at five years old. Before that, nothing.

I was raised in what seemingly appeared to be the average normal family. A mon and a dad. A house in the suburbs. A good school system. All the things that we want out of life. The reality is the truth was far from this. My father was an alcoholic and a pedophile. My mother was an enabler who was completely unwilling to deal with the truth. My brothers were the object of my father's affection as that was his preference, and I was just there.

I spent the majority of my days seemingly alone. I found solace in the library as each day after school, I went there to read books. Reading was my escape from reality. My mother babysat the neighborhood kids, and still, to this day, I cannot understand how the hours of 8-6 p.m. in my house seemed so normal and how after 7 p.m., everyday life was an inescapable horror.

In order to "escape," I learned how to hide. I learned how to make myself invisible. I remember spending hours upon hours hiding in my closet. I remember that the closet in my bedroom had two racks. One was all the way in the back, and it had older clothes and coats in it, and I could hide for hours, and no one would know where I was, and most of the time, if I was quiet, they didn't come looking for me. For the most part, I was just

113

there. There to figure out life for myself and there to constantly question my existence and why these people had me around in their family.

The issue with always hiding and escaping is the fear of being found and the reality of learning how to be sneaky, manipulative, and deceitful. My life was a shaky set of cards based on lies and half-truths. I never knew what to say to anyone because the truth was somewhere in the middle of the mess, so I became a master of deceit.

As a whole, my family was the definition of lies, misery, and deceit wrap up in a pretty package. Every day I see families all across America deal with these same issues. We wrap up our secrets and lives in various untruths and present ourselves and our families as perfect when the truth is far from that. As I was growing up and was faced more and more with the reality of my life, I vowed I would never live like this. I would become successful and have lots of money and live a life of freedom, but the truth is, in many ways, I became just like my mother. Unwilling to let the truth out, I lived in pain, misery, and lies for most of my life. It was easier to pretend to be happy instead of facing the truth.

My family situation at home became quite unbearable, and by the age of 13, I was placed in foster care and ended up in a group home. The group home I was in, back in Chicago in the '80s, was basically a prison for kids. Survival is your only mode of operation, and even the most innocent of children cannot escape the emotional damage of places like these. After several months and two different removals, I eventually ended up back in my adopted parents' care and back in their home.

All I could think about for years after this was how I could escape. This led me to lots of destructive behavior as a teenager. One thing I did realize was that I needed to at least get a high school diploma. I had made a promise to my 3rd-grade teacher that I would graduate from high school (for you teachers out there, know that your students hear you and will follow what you say, so always lead in love. You never know what a child is going through) and I intended to follow through with this promise.

Eventually, through many hurdles, homelessness, and teenage pregnancy, I graduated from High School and then graduated from college in 1996 and moved to Atlanta with my new husband, a man 13 years older than me I was "learning" how to love. I was now in a new state with my young son in tow, and I knew no one but him. The first few years were ok as we began to build a family and a business together. I worked so he could grow his company and take his earnings and reinvest it in the business so his company could prosper. I learned a lot about business from him. How to operate a company. What paperwork was needed. What the difference was between S and C corporations, LLC's and how they worked. I learned by doing and by helping him.

After about four years, his business began to flourish, and we began living the American dream. Big house in the suburbs, I was a stay at home mom, and everything looked perfect on the outside. Truth be told, the more my husband became successful, the more he felt that he had the right to do whatever he chooses with whomever he chooses to do it with. I was now faced with the decision to stay or leave. After many years of dealing with the emotional trauma and pain of this life, I decided to leave. Leaving came with a certain reality that for years I was fighting. The thought of being a single mom with now three children was terrifying. I had no idea what I was doing. I just knew that there had to be something else out there for me that was better than the pain of dealing with daily betrayal.

After leaving my marriage, I fell into everything possible under the sun to deal with the pain. It wasn't until just recently, almost 15 years later, that I finally dealt with the depths of my emotions as I figured out that every relationship that I had entered into after this was just a way for me to try to pay him back for what he had done to me. I put myself through additional trauma and pain to "payback" someone who didn't know I was doing this and most certainly didn't care.

How many of you go through this every day? We fight and damage our lives trying to pay back those who've hurt us. We search for others and things to make us feel good, and the cycle of hurt and pain continues. The truth is what we are really dealing with is the spirit of rejection. I believe this is the reason why so many of us hide our true selves and fall into traps of deception, which further exacerbates the lies and fallacies that we live in. The truth is we have to confront the spirit of rejection head-on and stop trying to mask the pain to get to the truth.

Here I was as an adult with a seemingly perfect life, back dealing with severe emotional rejection and pain. The spirit of rejection is rooted in the Orphan Spirit. The Orphan spirit is one that makes us believe that we are alone. I hid my pain for years because I felt alone, and no one was there to help me. I hid my shame of what was going on in my home because I didn't want anyone to know the truth. I wanted to keep up appearances. I loved feeling like my like was perfect. My kids were perfect. My husband was perfect when in truth, I was a married single mom with absolutely no foundation at all.

The Orphan Spirit and the Spirit of rejection keep us rooted in fear and shame and makes us think less of ourselves, which silences us and keeps us hidden in false prisms, never getting around to the truth of who we really are. The spirit of rejection (the fear of rejection) is the undertone to the orphan spirit as it causes us to operate in a place of perceived perfection as we try to hide our imperfections from others by masking our truth behind closed doors for fear of people knowing who we really are and what we are going through.

In order to run and hide, I have done it all!! I have sought every vice possible to hide from the truth. Sex, drugs, alcohol, relationships, organizations, anything and everything you could think of to try to find an acceptance. The spirit of rejection is tricky as it causes us to seek the very thing that hurts us. Our mind tells us to go do things that seemingly appear to be a way for us to win, but instead, they put us in a further place of defeat. This spirit of rejection is a never-ending spiral of trial and error. Failure is always lurking as we attempt to climb walls not meant for us to climb. We engage in destructive behavior, thinking we are winning when, ultimately, these things only harm us. The orphan spirit tells us to go. It's ok; he likes you. Go, it's ok; she's your friend. Go, it's all good; no one will find out.

Go, he deserves for you to treat him like that. Go, you are winning, when the truth is you are going down a path of destruction.

The spirit of rejection can be fought. It's fought by realizing that the opposite of rejection is acceptance, and there is only one way to be truly accepted, and that's through Jesus Christ. Acceptance doesn't come from people. Acceptance comes from God our Father, through Jesus Christ, our Savior, our King. The Orphan spirit lies to us daily, telling us that we do not have a home and that no one likes us. That we aren't good enough. Our answer and natural human defense is to prove it and everyone wrong, so we get up each day trying to outdo ourselves and each other. This spirit leads us into contention and bitter rivalries with others. It leads us, women, to compete with each other instead of coming together with a spirit of unity to edify one another. I believe this spirit is the reason for so much peril in our churches, communities, marriages, families, and relationships as we strive to compete instead of helping and complementing each other, so we all complete our assignments here on earth.

The truth is I was trying to run from rejection. By searching for acceptance, I was creating a false sense of hope in people and things hoping that this acceptance would take root and mask my pain. Unfortunately, I found out that the very thing I was searching for was bringing me things I didn't want. Rejection is a reality. People will reject you, and people will cause you pain. The truth is that even if people reject you, it's ok because we should not put our faith in people but instead put our trust, faith, and belief in Jesus Christ. He will never leave us or forsake us, so it's ok to face the reality of our lives because we are safe and supported in him. He will fix our pain and give us a new plan and a new purpose each and every time, so continue to put your trust in him.

Acceptance can only be found through Jesus Christ. He is the only way to find the truth and to be accepted by our Father, God! It took me 49 years, five days, and 6 hours to figure this out, and oh, what a blessing it is to know Jesus and know that I am truly accepted by him. I don't need to strive anymore to figure out where I belong. I belong in the kingdom of heaven, and I have found my home here with my brothers and sisters in Christ.

Finding acceptance through Jesus Christ helps us identify what is really important and, most importantly, deal with the people and circumstances in our lives. In Jesus Christ, even your failures will give you peace because the word of God states in Romans 8:28 "that God works all things together for the good of those who love him, who are called according to his purpose." Our acceptance that is found in Jesus lets us know that no matter what we face or what we do, or the circumstances that we have to live through, all of it works together for his plan and his purpose for our lives.

I still don't know much information about my birth or my life in my early years. What I do know is that God loves me. Jesus Christ has redeemed me, and he has a plan and purpose for my life that I cannot and will not hide from. I will live in the truth at all times. I will allow my life to be used by God for his plan and purpose, and I will fulfill the destiny that he has called me to, taking off the mask that I have worn, no longer hiding in shame but instead living in truth, in his name.

Today, take a moment to reflect on your past and see if you are holding on to any emotional baggage that is stopping you from living your best life. Remember, whoever you are trying to hurt by hurting yourself has probably long forgotten what they've done to you. Give yourself permission to let go and let God heal you and make you strong again so you can unmask your truth and walk in victory.

Kristen Fenrick is the founder of Disciples of Jesus Christ Ministries, Inc. As a successful entrepreneur and Woman of God, she is dedicated to helping others find their God-given purpose to live their best life in Christ Jesus. Finding your purpose is the ultimate goal for every believer. Getting past the pain and hurt is the first step. If you are looking for deliverance, it is there waiting for you in Jesus Christ. "Ask and it will be given to you, seek and you will find, knock and the door will be opened to you." (Matthew 7:7) Deliverance is right at the door for you, all you have to do is ask, and Jesus will answer you.

For more information about the ministry and finding your way to Jesus Christ, visit www.jesusloves.info. Jesus loves you no matter what you have done or experienced. You are loved!

About Kristen Fenrick

Kristen Fenrick is the owner of Klearly Kristen, Inc. a fashion jewelry and accessories brand and the host of EnStyle by Klearly Kristen a show that helps fashion, beauty and business entrepreneurs tell their story to her over 300M viewers on the new Promote-Her Network.

Kristen began her career in fashion back in 2015 as a way to help other women find their voice. As a former executive technology sales professional, Kristen understands the sacrifice it takes to make it in today's driven society. The idea behind her brand is to provide an opportunity for others to earn an income.

In early 2015 after deciding on ways to exit the corporate world, Kristen launched her jewelry business as a way to help others earn money to pursue their dreams. After pitching my ideas to various investors, I was told in order to proceed to the next level I would need to build my brand. I had no idea what that would entail however I took them on their challenge and decided that I would figure it out. At the time my money was running low and I had to decide what to do next. I had heard before that if you need something that you cannot afford to pay for, figure out what you can do to serve others and learn how to do it or create what you need for yourself. So, I did just that. I served and I learned and I mastered the fashion industry from the behind the scenes.

By working backstage, promoting events, and being a literal sponge, I've forged amazing connections that have allowed me to grow my brand which has now been featured with prominent brands on runways throughout the world. Now it's my time to give back to the industry I so dearly love.

EnStyle Fashion is designed to help you master the game. Our show has been developed to give fashion, beauty and business entrepreneurs a platform to showcase their work. Each week we will have special industry guest that will share their stories, triumphs and failures. We will spend time given valuable tips on how to expand your brand, increase your marketplace awareness and how to keep your business in order. We'll also have special guest such as artist, authors, health and wellness and inspirational faith-based individuals to pour into and grow you from the inside the out.

We are so excited to share our time with you each week! If you are interested in being a guest or a sponsor please reach out at the link below.

We're looking forward to spending time with you!

Love,

Kristen (put my heart signature here)

Klearly Kristen♡

PASTOR CONNIE LYONS

Beat a Retreat

Escaping the Snares of the Enemy

By: Pastor Connie Lyons

When I was a young teen, my dreams were utterly shattered after my mother was diagnosed with ovarian cancer. My mother had ten children, and I was the oldest child of the six younger children at home, and I helped my mother raise those siblings. My life began to tumble and became full of despair. I remember right before my 13th birthday, I visited my aunt in New York City. I looked up to her as a great inspiration, but I realized she was not a positive role model at all as I think back. I became very mischievous and started sneaking out of the house. By the time I was 15, my mother was getting sicker, and she was dying. I found the opportunity to sneak out of the house to have comfort because her life was slowly slipping away. I found comfort in spending time with my boyfriend, and I became pregnant.

As this beautiful life was growing inside me, my mom's life was drifting slowly away from me. My mom died in October 1980, and my daughter was born in November. My mother was my world, and I felt as if my life was over. I was a young mother at the age of 16, with no guidance. I was in the 10th grade; I loved school, ran track, and participated in several high school activities.

My aunt, whom I had great respect and admiration for in New York, would advise about life and how I could make my life easier. Her advice was, "you don't have to live in poverty; you have to use what you got to get what you want!" One of my older siblings took in the siblings that were home before my mother passed and took my daughter so I would be able to finish high school and start planning for our future. I was 17 and worked two jobs and got my own apartment to complete my education. I was baptized in the Catholic Church, and one of the nuns at my church encouraged me to stay in school, saying I was a special child of God even though I had a child out of wedlock and the community call me names and ridicule me, I should hold my head up and know that God had something special planned for me.

I graduated two years after my class, and the motivation that kept me going were the last words I heard my mom tell me "whatever you do, make sure you graduate, be something in life." I held those words near and dear to my heart, and I wanted her to be proud of me. I had to grow up fast, and I remember a song by Natalie Cole called Annie Mae. The older people in the community and some of my classmates called me Annie Mae because it was a song about a little girl that grew up too fast. I kept a smile on my face and had great expectations of being a dancer or choreographer on Broadway. I went to live in New York, and I lived there for three years with my aunt, who treated me like I was her daughter. All my dreams and expectations were crushed, I became very depressed; I was not accepted to dance school, and my aunt didn't have the money to pay for school.

I moved back home, but I felt lost and dying inside because I missed my childhood, and I began not to care about being a mother. I wanted to live free, and I found myself going to night clubs because I wanted to dance. Before I realized it, I was 27, dancing, partying, not taking responsibility for my child or my actions. When I turned 28, I hit rock bottom emotionally, things were going good financially, and I worked for the government and went to Beauty School. I met a drug lord who introduced me to fast money and easy life. The seed that was planted by my aunt was festering inside of me "use what you got to get what you want"! I was hooked on

the money, though I did not like the life and didn't know how to get out of it. I met my good friend, who talked to me about going to beauty school to become a licensed nail technician.

People look at me and say how wonderful I am and that I am such a beautiful woman of God, *yata, yata*. I am now, but back in the day . . .

I remember a time when I was living my life like it was golden, in 1996. It was when the cougar met the cub. His mom brought him in for a manicure for his graduation. He was fascinated and continued to visit me at my nail

124

salon. He asked to date me, but I told him he had to wait until he was 18. When he did, I became the ultimate present.

We partied, bought fancy clothes, cars, fine dining, and most of all, thought we were "In Love"! I say this not knowing destruction was in the midst. It was a ten-year span, and over these ten years, it was spoken into my life that I would minister to the broken spirited of women.

I worked for the government and owned a nail salon making lots of money, but it was never enough. The cub was fascinated by my luxurious lifestyle. I was 28, and he was 18, a senior in high school, so innocent, raised by his grandmother in the church with great morals. The promiscuous spirit deeply rooted inside me lusted over the innocent, vibrant youthfulness of that young man. My innocence was taken from me when I had a child at 16 years old. I missed out on all the fun things of growing up in high school, ball games, proms, dances, just being able to be a young, innocent girl. I took his innocence; this cub was fascinated and lusting over the cougar's youthfulness and experience, and that I owned a home and a luxury car.

Greed took over. I took him to the casino, and he got excited watching wealthy men gamble. When he turned 21, he had a gambling habit that was out of control. When he didn't have enough money, he started cooking crack cocaine and selling it. In the meantime, I was pushing myself away from him and yielding to the call and had a clear revelation of my destruction.

The relationship was severed due to the call to attend the school of ministry. We had no contact for years; I was on the straight and narrow, but because I was not delivered from the greed yet, he would dangle money from his gambling, and he used it as a lure. He called, and my past answered.

This is where my life could have gone to total destruction. I did not know my house was under surveillance for three years by the feds, and strangely enough, God's grace did not allow him to come to my house.

From the age of 21 to 25, the cub's gambling habits superseded the money he was making. He used grant money from going to beauty college, and it wasn't enough. His gambling habits were in excess of $20,000 to $50,000 on any given day.

I'm no longer in the relationship, but I felt shame for introducing him to the casino. I introduced him to a friend of the family who was a drug lord, and the cub began cooking crack cocaine to have money to feed his gambling addictions.

Years and years went by, and I'm constantly feeling an empty space because of my selfishness. I was constantly making my wrongs right, yet they were never right; they were always digging deeper into mass destruction for both of our lives. I was still being called by God, and his calming grace and mercy kept saving me.

Ten minutes and two exits later . . .

The cub called me at work and asked me to go to lunch and go shopping in New Orleans, and the greedy spirit of my past accepted the offer. He was 10 minutes and two exits away from me when he was stopped by the feds. He had two passengers in the car, and had I gotten into the vehicle, I would have gotten 10 years of day-to-day penitentiary time along with each one of them.

God's grace and mercy had covered me that day because I tried to call him to see where he was concerning picking me up and couldn't reach him. When he didn't show up, I continued working and later found out he was picked up by the feds. It's not easy being called; I went on and preached my initial sermon a year after he had spent a year in the penitentiary. I shared this testimony that day, and lives were changed because of God's grace superseding my flesh. I never had any contact with the cub the entire 10 years while he was in the penitentiary.

When he got out of jail, I asked for his and his family's forgiveness, and they did just as Jesus forgives. Forgiveness helped me to have a conversation with the cub that I ran the streets with and corrupted. I steered the path of his destruction instead of allowing him to make his own decisions in a positive way. Now we can talk to one another without the fear of regret and animosity. There are no lustful feelings or contentions of going back to that "old life."

God's grace surrounded me and changed me from being promiscuous and gifted me with a pastoral calling to help women not go down the same path that I went down. So many women get trapped with a drug lord and end up in the penitentiary or dead. I would like to help women understand that you reap what you sow; the lifestyle you think you want may cause you to end up in a place where it is a point of no return.

I made a promise to God because he saved my life that I will yield to the Holy Spirit. I will teach and help women who have gone to prison or are in prison because of bad relationship situations. I presently help a women's transition home with women coming out of the penitentiary or drug abuse, and I have ministered in the prisons.

My goals in life are to:

- Ensure women have resources to gain the help needed to help them transition into society
- Provide Counselors and Case Workers
- Teach them to be self-sufficient by providing skilled training

Teach them to love themselves and deal with the shame that will cause their demise

When it was prophesied to me as a young girl by the nun at church that God has something special planned for me, I now know His plan. I had a couple of near-death experiences where God had to wake me up face to face, a vision where I could choose death or the will of God through ministry. I asked God how could or why would he use a person like me because I didn't know the Bible very well, but I always had a love for God as a little girl. Matthew 19:14, Jesus said, "let the children alone and do not hinder them from coming to me; for the Kingdom of Heaven of belongs to such as thee."

God kept me from doing 10 years through his grace that stopped the vehicle 10 minutes, two exits away. Now I'm serving as an Outreach Pastor at Central Bible Church and The King's Kitchen, mother and mentor in my hometown. Presently, I am on WMEJ REJOICE 104.3 FM, where I am the Radio Director of Ministries and Founder/Speaker of Under The Olive Tree. A faithful member of the Ministers Alliance of Sisters on One Accord. Also, the PR Assistant of the Ezperanza Social Club.

I no longer struggle with a promiscuous spirit. God has anointed me with the gift of a pastoral ministry to broken women and men daily. I want my life to reflect the Grace of God by extending it to others. When the enemy knocks on my heart or mind and tells me I'm useless and worthless because of my past, I remind myself of my future; it's bright and a future of health and prosperity because I'm an overcomer. I'm living an abundant life according to Ephesians 3:20; I no longer carry the name of cougar. My new name is victory!

About Pastor Connie Lyons

Pastor Connie Lyons has been a minister for 12 years. She is a dynamic Woman of God, mentor, sister, and friend. She surrendered to God's calling on February 14, 2003 and Ordained to Pastor on December 28, 2008.

Pastor Lyons is under the leadership of Dr. Mike Ramsey and Lady Terri Ramsey at Central Bible Church located in Bay St. Louis, MS. She is the Outreach Pastor at The King's Kitchen and together, they are feeding and clothing the homeless and assisting in finding shelter while guiding them to a Bible-based ministry.

Presently, she is on WMEJ REJOICE 104.3 FM, where she is the Radio Director of Ministries and Founder/Speaker of Under The Olive Tree with Connie Lyons. She is a faithful member of the Ministers Alliance of Sisters on One Accord.

She has obtained a BA/Biblical Studies and is a Nail Technician from 1990 to present.

Although, Pastor Lyons has been recognized by many, her most celebrated accomplishment in life is being the mother of a beautiful daughter and 3 precious grandchildren.

Her life's journey has not been an easy one, but she is a survivor and surrounds herself with positive people and remaining steadfast in the word. Her favorite verse is Philippians 4:13 "I can do all things through Christ who strengthens me."

Contact and Follow Connie:

 +9853269146

 ecol7@yahoo.com

Personal
https://www.facebook.com/connie.lyons.395

Group
https://www.facebook.com/Under-The-Olive-Tree-with-Connie-Lyons-_1104802159563003/

Personal
https://www.instagram.com/utotministries/

Radio Broadcasts
https://m.rejoiceam1190.com/

RENA MARSHALL

A Close Call
By: Rena Marshall

God's call?

My call!

I've been to the point of no return twice in my life, and I didn't like who I was either time.

The first point of no return (let's call it A) was walking down the aisle with my dad in billowing white. So flowing and lacy and beautiful and committed was I and convinced by scripture and its promises that this marriage was what God wanted, and it was clear to my pounding heart that this was what I wanted too. There was no need to look for a return when all I wanted was this one-way ticket to love and bliss and children and happy ever after.

I was a nurse then, looking after others, and I righteously believed that *then* I was opening a loving door to the one person who would look after *me* as devotedly as I would look after him.

Little did I know that I *did* have that man in my life already.

My father.

And he was concerned.

As he walked me to my destiny (point A of no return), holding my hand, his expression told me he had a feeling. Not one of positivity, even though he loved me dearly that day and every day, but one of foreboding. It seems he was as unsure of my husband as I was sure, and he tried to gently warn me about it in a joking way.

Walking down the aisle, my father whispered, 'Now why do you want to get married again? You don't have to do this. Let's turn around, and I promise you no-one will bother you.

133

I whispered back, 'Dad, we're in church, behave. I looked over the congregation and caught the eye of an elderly lady I respected and who would always scold dad and me for talking and giggling in church. As if God didn't like a bit of humor now and again!

Dad wasn't finished (lucky it was a long aisle, and we were walking slowly). 'Look, I told you before; you don't need to get married. Just go on and finish college. I also know of *his father*' (by Dad's face, I could guess *his father* was something about which he'd rather not have known). We were both smiling at people in our whispery walk. Miss Naïve, me, stopped Daddy by saying, "Everyone is different").

We pressed on, him squeezing my hand and me squeezing his back, 'you play too much, Daddy.' (Time would come when playing at a happy marriage, smiling through the pain, became what I was trying to do every day, I'd realize he wasn't playing at all) Headstrong, just like Daddy, audacious and opinionated too, I wanted what I wanted. So we kept on walking.

And on that long-awaited day, Daddy and I pressed forward, then at the altar hugged, a loving look in both our tear-filled eyes and his kiss on my forehead, the whisper strengthened to those fateful words.

'Yes, I give this bride away.'

Eight years later, I wanted to give my husband away.

In the beginning, we were happy. Years of married and family life trickled through the hourglass. Movie night, late-night talks, dancing, beach visits, frequent family and friends' gatherings, playing cards, fun abounded. Harmony peppered with a little indifference was be expected.

All was good if you could open your heart to let go of what happened the day before. And focus on the days to come.

When I wasn't working as a qualified nurse practitioner (my second degree after my first Bachelor of Science), I kept us, as a couple, and our family positive, juggling our lives with church and fun activities. Keeping my husband and me happy and tending to our time together and time with our children occupied my waking, non-working hours.

In an effort to alter negative family dynamics and build self-esteem, I would pour in experiences, bringing the kids, family members and other children that would frequently be around us to museums, musicals, adventure parks, indoor activities and educational but fun sites. I explored what I saw delighted my kids and supported their dedicated interests - rock/gem collections, coin collections, purse collections, dance, ballet, pop warner cheerleading, piano, singing, backyard picnics, and the like.

Alternating big vacations for the kids one year and the next for us as a twosome was a family custom. Taking vacations is something I love so much more than shopping. So it also helped me. Vacations were met with obstacles from my husband until I decided I was going anyway, with my spouse or without him.

Thanks to Daddy and his encouragement of my daring side, that turned into, 'well I'm coming,' and my husband began to learn why I enjoyed exploring the world. He then followed to the Bahamas, Hawaii and various other places alternating choices for everyone. Enhancing what the kids learned in school that year was done by traveling to some of those places or something similar to augment their education.

My daughter and I traveled with a gospel singing group, the YYAFA out of Silsbee Texas, singing at the White House and others, and my oldest even sang at Carnegie Hall with her school choir. She was old enough to participate and remember. All of these involvements were a golden opportunity to show my children and family various experiences and see the United States and the world with a purpose. Bringing the church's youth department to retreats and various places was also inspiring me to give back to the community.

Nevertheless, trying to introduce various forms of family time, separate and apart from our children, did not stop the incoming avalanche of spousal differences that I saw coming. I leaned on counseling, positive, mature couples, church elders, and most of all, God.

Of course, nothing is perfect. I found that hard to accept when I realized that there weren't many resources to turn to for guidance, whether you're old or young in the relationship. Mom's molded and dad's sweet potato pie baby girl sought to find a way to navigate this differently and have a personal truth about the situation. Thank God for mom's grooming, for my personality trait took more after Dad's audacity and fearless stance first vs. mom's more humble quiet spirit. After much prayer, spousal dialogue, sessions of counsel from both spiritual leaders and professionals outside of the church, issues subsided.

So did the good times. Attempts to bring them back were frequently met with a lack of interest.

I felt my marriage begin to falter despite all my intervention and loving support.

I looked personally for help in 2 places.

God.

And inside myself.

Meanwhile, in Texas, gas doesn't just run your car; it runs your life.

And my husband, being a contractor in the petrochemical industry, had a work record that went up and down with the petrol price. Soon our marriage followed the same bumpy path.

Eight years down the road, our marriage ran out of gas.

We faced turmoil and disharmony after years of intermittent work with my spouse, who did not work regularly, and with me working full-shift and studying to improve our income over time.

Twelve-hour shifts became my norm from 7 am to 7 pm one week, to 7 pm to 7 am the next week. I was exhausted with my house to run, my kids to raise, my husband being unhelpful and demotivated by his fluctuating work schedule, my immune system turned inside out by shiftwork, stress-related hypertension becoming the order of the day, and at worst, periods of 72 hours without sleep.

Church people, following their interpretation of scripture (why didn't I remind myself that it was *my* interpretation that mattered, it was *my* God and *my* life), said stay in there.

You're the one covering your family - keep on doing it.

So I did.

It's what's best for the kids at this breaking point, I thought.

Arguments escalated, and my husband began to hit out.

The blows landed on me.

Domestic violence filled my home with physical fights and other acts of torment.

In my mind, I wasn't built to break, and so fighting back became the norm.

I rationalized using the saying, "hurt people hurt people." My quest to understand brought me to research that shared instances of hurt feelings, bullying, resentfulness, or acting out negative behavior towards others may stem from the individual feeling inadequate or less powerful than another. But as they de-value their spouses, family or another person, the perpetrator also has an internal devaluation.

Or maybe he thought I was going to stay through all the turmoil, just as our parents did.

Studies showed that children from a two-parent home adjust better in life. But studies also show what harm regular domestic violence can do to the family members exposed to it.

I could either remain under the physically abusive control of another or leave. I really felt trapped for my kid's sake, spiritually and physically.

Choices became poor because I barely slept. I began using additional tactics of meditation, counseling. My counselor was afraid for me and encouraged me to get a taser since I was afraid of a gun. (Later in another life, I'd overcome that fear).

If my husband wasn't whole, and Lord knows I felt so much less of a person after being hit on, neither of us was whole. My children needed wholeness, and I was the one to see to it.

There was only one right way to wholeness at this point B of no return.

I filed for divorce.

He would come around my job early in the mornings and wait for me in the parking lot, bringing the drama there. I would go into my job upset, but as the house supervisor, I could stay in my office a while to recoup before engaging with the staff. Eventually, security noticed, and they began paying attention to my moves on camera for my safety because I was mainly alone most of the time, moving around the hospital at night—a rather large building with many inconspicuous spots for someone to hide.

People did not know about the fighting, except for a few family and friends.

Friends and family were alarmed when a police officer shot and killed his wife after a courthouse dispute, and I received warning calls because they didn't want the same thing to happen to me. After actually leaving, but before the divorce was completed, things got worse.

They say an abuser is at his most violent around the time he's been left.

I was followed to most places that I went to. If I had a car in my driveway that he did not know, he began lurking. Some male friends would check on me and let me know when they discovered him watching the house.

Mandatory hurricane evacuation ensued, and he came to take my car from the kids and me, leaving us with no way of escaping, as we were supposed to. A brother stepped in to make him leave at gunpoint. Another brother stepped in and began to hang out more around my house to ward him off after finding out all I was going through.

A series of fearful events followed, the most public being when he stalked us and dragged me by the hand into my car, taking my keys. Then he reached past the kids to hit me. The police were called by the friends I was visiting, and the 'hi-jacking' threat was resolved.

I was saddened for my children because even though they had witnessed some of the fighting, they still ran to their dad like he was a hero. I called him "the great manipulator." If you didn't know the truth of a situation, he could twist it for his benefit. So I had to find a way to understand that if he could manipulate and charm his way back into my life, he could certainly mislead the children.

Years later, I was charmed into dating him again because he wanted his family back. He began helping with the kids more and spending quality time. Although I remained skeptical for a while, he had even convinced some of my staff that he had changed, talking to them, buying some of them late-night lunch and bringing it up for us.

So I married him again.

I was convinced by him that he had changed. He'd become more active in the church and committed to living a Christ-like life. So down the aisle, we went again. But I emphasized one thing. That if he ever started the fighting again, I would be out of the marriage much quicker than the last time.

It took three years, and again, I filed for divorce. A woman of my word. If not my church's word.

But it took a little more time because he had convinced my youngest daughter that I was trying to break up the family. He convinced her that I didn't love her and that he did, so she wanted to live with him. I wasn't able to persuade her otherwise. He even led her to believe that I put her in all her private lessons because I didn't want to be bothered with her, not that I was helping her be well-rounded like her big sister.

A horrible strand of manipulation that wound itself around my aching heart.

(And of course, who had to get everyone to their various destinations but me?).

My better judgment in this painful issue was that parents who pulled their kids in different directions resulted in the children being the ones to suffer the hurtful consequences.

I've been to the point of no return twice in my life with A and B, and I didn't like who I was either time. There was nothing that could stop me from getting to the person who was repeatedly bothering me when I asked him to leave me alone.

Shivering with fear, slightly more for the gun than the abuser, I went to a gun store to buy one.

'I need a gun to stop a person if they come towards me fighting,' I told the helpful shop assistant.

'Not a little girlie gun, one with hollow points like I've seen on TV. Maybe I could damage a leg or something. But not too much noise because guns scare me so.'

He realized I was a complete novice and a frightened one, and he gently showed me how to shoot and load. He put in 2 bullets for me.

One scary husband, two bullets, and a shaking hand. Would this new point of no return end with me in jail?

Luckily, divorce, a second one for veteran me, was the shot through his heart instead.

Now, no gun intended, my kids are grown, and living well is my best revenge.

About Rena Marshall

Rena Marshall is a mother of 3, 2 girls, a nephew and 8 grandchildren. I love, love, love spending time with my family and mostly… the grandkids. My hobby is singing, traveling, dancing and helping people. I never meet a stranger and willingly communicate with people.

In the past, I have owned and operated a children's apparel store. This started as a hobby and was something I really enjoyed. Managing funds, organizing, categorizing, going to market, and developing a great advertisement forum for this business was a great accomplishment for me.

Presently, I have a Master's in Nursing. Also, two bachelor's degrees are held, Bachelor of Arts and Applied Sciences with a business focus and a Bachelor of Science in Nursing- Registered Nurse / Certified Clinical Documentation Specialist of many years. Presently auditing the physician's/ medical providers to optimize documentation of care given, revenue opportunities and compliance with regulatory boards. I have worked in various leadership capacities from clinical nursing at the bedside to hospital administrator. My professional memberships are of the Texas Nurses Association and the American Nurses Association. Membership of the Healthcare Compliance, Regulation, and Management organization (HCPRO) is also body of certification participation.

From 1996 – 2002, I was on the Texas Health and Human Services Commission Medical Care Advisory Committee Member- Medicaid Division. This is a federally mandated state committee that recommends operations of the Medicaid Program for the State of Texas.

An instructor for Advanced Life Support (ACLS) was an additional role from 1989-2002. During the summer of 1998, I went to Europe as a presenter and assisted in conducting discussion groups on European and American Healthcare during a study abroad through Lamar University, Beaumont Texas.

Foreign Mission to Haiti since 1998 on an annual and bi-annual basis is also a part of my life experiences. This included assisting in coordinating and going to the foreign territory to fulfill this in-kind volunteer ministry. Means of support were financial, food and hands on for selfcare, clean water safety techniques, a well was built for log-term clean water access, wellness / medical assessments with treatment including medications, medical clinic built and stocked; Academic and Christian education for various ages, staff and pastoral support, Arts development with donation of instruments to school.

In the past I was an Executive / Advisory Committee Member and instructor for a foundation called Educating, Supporting, and Building Character (ESBC). This foundation was developed to prevent teenage pregnancy, teach post-natal care, and build character to the youth. A program funded by the March of Dimes.

I am a member of Lilly Grove Baptist Church of Houston Texas, participating in the Choir, Sunday school and yet still- Foreign mission. Before I moved to Fresno, I participated in my church in various capacities such as: Foreign Mission, Choir member, Youth Department Educator and Assistant Director, Youth Matron of Liturgical Praise Dancer's and Coordinator of Workshops for the Golden Triangle, Jefferson County at Eastern Star Baptist Church from 1998 to 2007.

My goal is to continue participation in the support of our community, world and to grow personally, professionally and spiritually.

Rena Marshall

DR. SYLVIA MOLO JONES

AS IS

I am Woman, Mother, Mate (MWM)

By: Dr. Sylvia Molo Jones

Place your hand over your heart. Can you feel your heartbeat? YAY! You are alive. You are breathing, and that is a good thing!

When I look back over my life and think about my lived experiences, I can truly say, "all is well. I have lived and am living a good life."

As my journey continues to unfold, I am compelled to share a snippet of a few moments that altered my life. To become a dentist, what I thought was my life work turned out to be nothing I would have imagined due to the ups and downs with my education. I thought I would literally be creating and caring for smiles—well, not. That thought became a real-life lesson called surrender.

What I will share here is an opportunity for you to identify with your own life journey and where you thought a thing, a process, a journey would be, and then where an "as is" entered in.

Woman, I am a female. A woman.

I did not get to decide this; however, I am grateful that God made me a woman, from a wound of man.

W—Woman—a "grown woman," that I am. I need a t-shirt.

Have you ever been shopping and seen an item with the tag that says, "as is?" I purchased an item with a tag that read "as is," and it spoke to me. It had me take a picture of the tag. It spoke to me the way the Holy Spirit spoke to me in 1997. I was a woman on a mission to be active in my career as a dentist. That in itself is a whole story. Well, I had a best friend practicing dentistry in Houston, Texas. My family and I had moved back to

145

Houston, and we had a newborn. My husband was serving in ministry at a church that also had a school, and for whatever reason, one day, he came home and asked me to stay home.

Stay home?

"Stay home with Asha," he said. I questioned him to find out how and why he asked me this or actually "stating" this. Bottom line, he did not want Asha to attend school. She was a baby, he thought, so she was not ready for school. He was thinking ahead and envisioning her life and her life in school. I, on the other hand, was listening while envisioning my life at home. What? Wait? Not!

In the next week or so, I prayed, journaled and read the scriptures. All these things are vital in my being. I knew that question? The "statement" deserved an answer. An answer not from my feelings, not from my flesh, and certainly not from my thoughts of my funds. The answer had to come from a true place of life-giving substance. The answer had to come from a deeper level of myself, and only God could manifest that through me. I clearly remember where I was when the answer appeared. Yes, it appeared as I was in the mirror trying on hats. Church hats. I was going to wear a hat to church, and I was standing in my bathroom mirror looking at myself, and I clearly heard the Holy Spirit say, "I will use you as is." I looked in the mirror closely. Do y'all do mirror work? Well, that's a whole thing. Anyhoo, I leaned in closer to the mirror and responded with, "okay??"

I knew this would be a conversation for my journal, and I know I wrote that "as is" statement and re-wrote that and stayed with that for a while. "As is." Spending time in prayer, spending time journaling, and spending time reading scripture. Repeat. I stayed with it, and then I heard this, "ministry will provide for you, not dentistry." To that, I said, "WHAT? Oh, My Goodness!!!"

At this time, my husband was not home yet, and I was walking around, saying that out loud. Oh, you don't do that? Talk out loud to yourself? Well, that's a whole thing too! I kept repeating what I heard and praying out loud and thinking, Oh My Goodness! How am I going to share this with my Mom?

That was my next question? My Mom had invested in my educational journey—my whole life journey. Once she embraced me not practicing dentistry, I was good. I had to share what was revealed to me with her and repeat it a few times over several weeks until it could settle a bit. It had a sting to it. It was a surrender like none other because my journey had been long and interesting. I had attended not one dental school but two. I did not attend school in-state but out of state too. Can you say,

"As is."

M—Mate. I said, "Yes!" Now, I am a wife.

He asked, and I said, "Yes!" I married my high school sweetheart, and we are approaching thirty years of becoming one.

Did I know what I was saying yes to? Well, I thought of one, two, three things, maybe four things. I certainly did not think about ALL these things! These amazing life and love lessons I have learned from being a helpmate have grown me into the woman I am today. With this assignment, I have found that by intentionally participating in our relationship, by attending a marriage retreat every year of our marriage, I am a good mate if you ask me. We have been engaged in marriage ministry from our first year of marriage until the present. We were told we would be serving in the marriage ministry at our new church in a new city, and we had not been married a year yet. Did I say our first year of marriage? God had a plan. "As is." We journeyed with many couples in Missouri, and when we returned to Texas, we continued sharing in marriage ministry. We eventually started a 501(c)3 not-for-profit that has touched many marriages. It has its own place in relationships, a standing date of the first Friday of every month.

As the helpmate, I am still processing many things. I get to share life with the love of my life, and we are becoming one. I believe that takes forever. As I view how-to's? How to do this. How to say this. How not to do or say this! Yikes! I am encouraged by my journey to my "as is."

Now, remember, he was the one who asked the question? "Will you stay at home with my baby." I now cannot imagine my life if he had not asked the question and if I had not taken it seriously. The question shook me. It shook my comfort. It shook my core. It shook what I thought I knew to become my truth. I had planned my dental career for sixteen years. I had attended two dental schools, and I had graduated with dental school debt. Debt! What? Stay home? Become a stay-at-home Mom. You may recall, for whatever reason, the conversation at the time in the late nineties was about stay-at-home Moms versus go-to-work Moms. It was a thing. I have been processing that from the day I made the decision to stay until now. To stay home was the choice that changed everything.

WooHoo! We have come this far by love, respect, prayers, tears, joys, faith and BUNCHES of Laughs.

As is.

M—Mom. I became one in two ways. First, by saying, "Yes," to the question, "Will you marry me?" Secondly, by giving life from my womb. Now, I am a mother.

So, because I was clear about becoming a Mom the same day I became a wife, I did not have plans for any more children. My bonus baby was perfect, "as is." My husband agreed with the plan, so at the time, he shared it. The second I shared with him that I heard the voice of the Lord say, "it's time?" He was ready! He had been ready to have more children. That was not in my plans. My bonus baby was plenty.

It's time to what, for what I asked? Holy Spirit responded, "Have a baby." This conversation was occurring in church, approximately 8:20-ish a.m. I was sitting on a pew all by myself. After church, I shared this with my husband, and the journey began immediately, just like that. SuperNatural ChildBirth is what I named it. It was simply amazing. And it happened again, just like that. SuperNatural ChildBirth. That, too, is a whole story.

As is.

As I have processed through my life being me. Self-accessing me has been weaved throughout my life. Developing my thought processes, evolving in every area; woman, mate, mom, and growing in my faith has been vital in this "as is" movement. I have applied lessons learned along my journey, adjusting along to bring me to this moment. Now, I stand looking over my life, knowing I have lived a good life. The surrendering led to a greater good for all. I surrendered to an assignment greater than myself, and I have received blessings greater than the things I thought I would create for myself. What I know is everyone has an "as is" moment. Pay attention.

What's yours? When God says to you, "I will use you as is." How do you respond? How did you respond? As the woman or man you are, how will your gifts be used in this time? Will the surrendering be something you have prepared for, planned for, and be the thing that propels you to a higher good. The smiles I see daily in my family cannot compare to the smiles I would have created or cared for with the skills I learned in school. The life skills I learned from my being present to myself, present to my spouse, and present to my daughters have manifested an unspeakable joy. Now, when I look back over my life and think things over, I can truly say that I have been shaken and I have been, and with that, I am an all in AS IS GIRL! I see the good. I speak the good. And I am the good that spreads joy and light. I am embracing my amazing life like never before, and I pray that as I share this message, this movement of staying with yourself and identifying what tools you have to serve you in assessing you will cause you to pause. Listening is required. I have found that self-assessment has been my greatest work. Applying that which will serve me is the key. Whining, complaining, and negativity woulda, coulda, shoulda, had no place in the goodness that was to come for me. I would not have known if I had not listened and applied my truth despite what it looked like to myself and others. Being me ~ AS IS. This is a daily work. Surrendering. Listening. Applying. That's a whole thing!

Nothing can stop me.

AS IS

Always seeking.

Seeking always.

I

See.

AS IS.

~Sylvia Molo Jones

About Dr. Sylvia Molo Jones

Sylvia M. Jones is a leader with a servant's heart. Sylvia attended Prairie View A&M (1988) and University of Missouri – Kansas City School of Dentistry (1996). She has been empowering relationships since 1991. She is the founder of Woman Mate Mother (MWM) and SMJ, III, Consultants.

Sylvia is a retired dentist who loves to see people smile! Her mission is to believe, express, and serve truth to herself and others. Honesty and authenticity and a few things others share about her. Her purpose is to position people and she does this effortlessly. In positions as a spouse, parent, Spiritual Director and Chaplain she recognized her gifts of shepherding and praying as vital tools, supporting others on their journey.

Sylvia has been married to her high school sweetheart Ed Jones for 29 years and they have three "adultish" daughters. Sylvia loves her family, her friends, and people, all people. She does not meet strangers, she meets you.

Sylvia's training in listening allows her to use her God-given gifts to support others. In her vision experience workshops she walks with you in seeing a reality beyond your current situation and does it so well because she did it for herself.

YVONNE TIMS

The Impact of a Child

By: Yvonne Tims

I am told I talk a lot, but that is because I have been living for so long. I am full-up with life stories, my own story, as well as my clients' stories. Today, at the grand old age of 82, I am the oldest of 10 children, a mother of 5, and a two-time cancer survivor. I cherish the opportunity that God has blessed me with to share my story. I hope my stories can draw comfort, knowledge, and understanding.

My life story took a less-travelled turn in the turbulent '60s. I was married at 18 with a husband in the military. I had three children when I met an angel with colorless eyes named Jane. I say she has colorless eyes because Jane was not the same color as I, but you would have never known it by the way she treated me.

Jane was a 9-year-old white girl, daughter of a doctor in our town. I was Black, hired to be her nanny because of her terminal illness of which she had not been told. In the beginning, the doctors thought she had rheumatoid arthritis. They said she would be over it within a year. Then, spots started showing up on her body and her hair started falling out. She had leukemia. I knew that she was aware of her illness and that she knew that I was aware of it. We never talked about it, although to this day, I wish we had. She would ask me to read the obituaries to her daily. She would ask what symptoms came with heart disease, diabetes, etc. It was like she was trying to diagnose herself. She asked how it felt to die. One day, I took her to the cemetery upon her request. She told me what kind of flowers she wanted at her funeral. She was transforming from a child to an adult right in front of my eyes. Medical attitudes were guarded then. The truth was not necessarily shared with the patient, especially a child. Jane's mother appeared to be numb when coping with her daughter's illness.

Racial attitudes and tensions were rampant in Mississippi at the time. Civil rights were not yet on the table. Black domestic workers could not use the bathroom in a white home, nor could they eat at the table with white families. The same restriction applied to nannies, but it did not apply to me. It was a struggle for us Black Americans who worked as nannies for white families to step over the indignity and disrespect of racism mixed in with the very natural and abiding love we felt for their children.

I was treated like family by Jane and her mother. Her father, who came from ancestors of anti-black organizations, was not so warm in the beginning. He forbade that I sit in the front seat when taking me to the bus stop due to embarrassment and did not allow me to sit at the table. Jane united us all. She told her family that no one could help the fact that God made me black. From that point on, her father learned to respect me. Jane and I grew a loving relationship that had nothing to do with color and everything to do with being human.

The Impact of Death

Keeping the fact that a little girl was dying right in front of me was hard. I respected her family's wishes, and along with them, I kept Jane from knowing the most important thing about her life—that it was not going to last a year from then. I tried to make the last year the best years of Jane's life. I would sing her favorite lullaby daily: Danny Boy. I knew this young girl, a child, was preparing herself for death. I was not hired just to be her nanny, but to be the person her soul attached to on this earth.

I was so angry when Jane died. The church had a set time that they prayed for Jane to get better. Everyone joined together in worship to pray her back to health. When she failed to get better, and eventually died, I got mad at God. I questioned why and how He could let such a young child die. I did not go to church for 15 years. For a religious woman like me, that was quite out of the ordinary. I was hurt, confused, and above all deeply saddened by the loss. Through all of this, the Lord did not leave me. God had a plan. Nothing happens by chance. I can say with confidence and conviction that I do what I do today because of God's plan and Jane. She saw in me what I could not see in myself. She lived a lifetime in the last 9 months of her life and told me to make it a point to help others in their times of need. Jane told me that I had a responsibility to spread happiness to the children and people I encountered. That was a tall order, but I have filled it.

God shapes us in our darkest moments. He defines our very lives in times of discomfort. Little did I know that the young child whose condition I was saddened by was shaping me to be the helper I am today. Had I not experienced the goodness that was Jane, or the innocence of one accepting death, I may not be as impactful to the lives of people I encounter today. For all of this, I am truly grateful.

Pain can be buried for a lifetime and pushed under the mat along with all the injustices one might have encountered surrounding it. Jane died in front of me. That was one of the hardest moments for me. I am often asked by those grieving, "why did my loved one go when I wasn't in the room?" My answer is, "because they wanted to spare you and go on their own." If a person is not there, they were not meant to be there. Someone who is passing will know who can handle their oncoming passing and who cannot.

I credit all 5 of my children, including the three that were with me during the time I took care of Jane. My children provided loving attention, continuous affection, and busy, interesting activities for helping me through my down time after Jane. They did not know the whole story, but filled the void, nonetheless. When I was home with them, my close-knit family made all the difference. I did my best to hide my sadness for their sake. As the old saying goes, life must go on. This meant the same for me, even if Jane were not there to share it. I attribute my time with Jane to my success as a Grief Counsellor, Social Worker, and Substance Abuse Counsellor. I know from my psychology and social work that pain can be buried for a lifetime and pushed under the mat along with all the injustices one might have encountered surrounding it.

The Impact of Moving Forward

After Jane passed, I started my journey of helping children by becoming an assistant teacher at Head Start. I later enrolled at Jefferson Davis Jr. College, now known as Mississippi Gulf Coast Community College. I was one of three Black students in the College's integration program. It was not easy being one of just three, so I put my head down and did what I had to do.

After junior college, I enrolled at the University of Southern Mississippi for a bachelor's degree in Pre-professional Psychology. I was on my way to helping both children and adults. I went as far as obtaining two Master's Degrees: one in Community Counselling and the other in Social Work both from the same Alma Mater. I started walking further into my purpose and became a licensed Master's Level Social Worker in Louisiana and Mississippi and a Licensed Chemical Dependency Counsellor. Today, I am a Licensed Chemical Dependency Counsellor in Texas.

During grade school, one of my many treasured memories of this transformational time was standing up to bullies in my community, a skill learned harder by but essential as a mother and a social worker. I learned from my bully management that I had to be brave to stand up to those throwing their weight around and stand up for those who could not fend for themselves. I fought back. At the same time, I needed to work out a strategy to convert the bully. With a blend of understanding and decisive action, I was able to bring about change in a bully's behavior.

I saw the need to rescue many people I came across in my earlier life who were bullied by circumstances, who believed themselves to be of little value. Some were substance abusers, had low self-esteem. Some were depressed children or adults who had given up on themselves. I not only saw their potential but was able to help them to see it too. Everyone deserves to be picked up when they fall. I remember all their stories as if they were my own. Their stories could have easily been mine had I not been goal-oriented, motivated, competitive, educated, and enlightened by my family ethics growing up. My parents never finished high school, but every single one of my nine siblings has an education.

I pride myself on being a fighter for the underdog and have done just that in my lifetime. I filed a complaint with the Federal Oversight Agency in Washington, DC against goods and services designated for underprivileged children. Then, there was my work with Veterans. I fought for military men more used to fighting for their country than fighting for themselves. I took up their cause and battled for their rights as a Social

Worker appointed for the Department of Veteran Affairs, liaising between them and the Veteran Administration to introduce – my big oxygen moment - designated smoking areas. I was the voice that brought about change to the administration on behalf of the Veterans.

Music can heal the soul. It is a gift that I have been blessed to share with the world around me as a vocalist. I have been playing with different bands including a medley of music for quite some time and proudly use music in my techniques. The musical skills came in useful in my counseling rooms—it was inspiring and healing. Grief counseling for those encountering major loss is my strength, and the clients I have counseled felt relief within 24 hours after one of my sessions that included music to motivate and encourage. While at Jeff Davis, I provided music. I have hosted a blood drive with my band live on the news. In 1984, I represented Mississippi at the World Fair in New Orleans as one of 54 competing acts. I am listed as Blues artist for the state of Mississippi in the Blues Roundup. I have a recorded song called "Blues Always".

One last bully that could have led to grief for me was Cancer. Again, I took a strong stand and got the better of Pancreatic Cancer and Gastric Cancer by being cheerful whenever I could (*never let the bully get the better of you*), taking an interest in my fellow patients (*a Social Worker's never off duty*), and seizing the day for immediate surgery— 'How soon can I operate?' asked the surgeon. 'Just as soon as you can book an operating theatre,' I replied. I beat the bully and am living in remission and continuing to help others.

And now I end my story and remember Jane. The bottom line is she led me to where I am today. I know she is looking down on me. I did it, and I will continue to do so. I sing Danny Boy, stand up for those who cannot stand up for themselves, and fight any bully that comes around.

About Yvonne Tims

Yvonne is the elder of 10 children born to the union of David and Ruthan Jefferson. She was born in Arms, Mississippi on July 2,1938. Yvonne attended China Lee Baptist Church and sang in the choir

After graduating from the 8th grade in China Lee, Yvonne transferred to McCullum High School and excelled in Basketball. Yvonne was a competitor with confidence to go against the best; Infact, she bumped a senior for starting position as a freshman. Yvonne has a history of being ambitious, goal oriented, reliable in her endeavors. This is evident in courage to stand up to bullies in her community, one of three Black to integrated Jefferson Davis Jr College when her fourth child was 9 months old. Yvonne took a stand against goods and services designated for the under privileged children by filing a complaint with Federal Oversight Agency in Washington, Dc. Yvonne was appointed the liaison between veterans and the Veteran Administration that resulted in designated smoke areas. Yvonne provided guidance in the veteran's voices being heard by the administration.

As a social worker and community counselor, Yvonne is noted for working with persons other professionals place little or no value. Yvonne treated substance abusers, depressed children, adults years ago who are fully functioning years later. Yvonne exhibits respect, enthusiasm, attentiveness and caring attitude whether in a personal or professional capacity.

A person who has experienced death or a major loss usually feels better within 24 hours of the first counseling session. Yvonne uses music to motivate her clients. She has an extensive background as a vocalist with bands that played a variety of music. Yvonne is a trailblazer as indicated by achieving what she aspires in life. She makes the sacrifice to obtain a goal.

Yvonne earned two master's degrees from the University of Southern Mississippi and was employed as social worker for the Department of Veterans Affairs, Memorial Behavioral Health, The Regional Center, Long Beach, Miss. Also, she was employed as a counselor by Gulf Coast Mental

Health Center and Gulfport Head start, Employment in Houston, Texas include Substance counselor for Santa Maria Hostel, Riverside Hospital, Houston Alcohol and Drug Council, The Harris Center. Yvonne is employed part-time for Trade It in and Enlightenment Family Services

She is family oriented and spends quality time with her 5 children Yvonne is divorced from her husband and father of her children. An example of Yvonne's faith is her positive attitude that helped her survive stage 2 pancreatic and gastric cancer in 2017. Yvonne is cancer free and wowed her medical staff with her smile and will to live.

Credentials

BS Degree in Pre-professional Psychology

Master's Degrees in Community Psychology and Social Work

Licensed Chemical Dependency Counselorand in the process of applying for renewal of Licensed Master's level Social Worker in Louisiana and Mississippi

Made in the USA
Monee, IL
20 March 2021

62572008R00098